T0058112

101
Bass Fishing Tips

101
Bass Fishing Tips

Twenty-First Century Bassing Tactics and Techniques from All the Top Pros

JOHN NEPORADNY, JR.

Skyhorse Publishing

Skyhorse Publishing books may be purchased in bulk at special discounts for sales promotion, corporate gifts, fund-raising, or educational purposes. Special editions can also be created to specifications.

For details, contact the Special Sales Department, Skyhorse Publishing, 307 West 36th Street, 11th Floor, New York, NY 10018 or info@skyhorsepublishing.com.

Skyhorse® and Skyhorse Publishing® are registered trademarks of Skyhorse Publishing, Inc.®, a Delaware corporation.

www.skyhorsepublishing.com

10 9 8 7 6 5 4 3 2

Library of Congress Cataloging-in-Publication Data is available on file.

ISBN: 978-1-62087-792-0

Printed in China

Contents

Introduction

When insurance salesman Ray Scott held the First All-American Invitational Bass Tournament June 6–8, 1967, on Beaver Lake in Arkansas, he changed the world of bass fishing.

Before those 106 anglers gathered at Beaver Lake to fish the first ever cash-prize tournament, bass fishing was a leisurely weekend pursuit enjoyed by a smattering of anglers mostly from the South. In the last four decades, the increasing popularity of bass tournaments has turned the sport into a multibillion dollar industry enjoyed by millions of anglers throughout the United States and in a handful of foreign countries around the world.

During the early days of Scott's Bass Anglers Sportsman Society (BASS), only a small group of guides and serious competitive anglers fished professionally. Today most of the contestants on the Bassmaster Elite Series and FLW Tour circuits are full-time professionals who help educate the bass fishing public through seminars, videos, podcasts, and magazine and newspaper articles.

The influence of competitive bass fishing on the angling industry is comparable to NASCAR's impact on the automobile industry. The same technology used to create lighter, faster race cars is being copied by the auto industry to improve fuel efficiency and increase safety features in the vehicles we drive every day. The pros on the tournament circuits have also proven to be invaluable test pilots for tackle manufacturers and boat builders, as these competitive anglers spend countless hours fishing in the sun, rain, wind, cold, or heat, navigating in high waves or making long runs at full speed to reach remote hotspots. Their exploits in all sorts of weather and water conditions have helped fishing companies create more durable, dependable tackle and boat manufacturers build safer and stronger bass boats.

Every major fishing tackle company and bass boat manufacturer have filled their pro staff teams with the best anglers from the national circuits, because these companies know the time the touring pros spend on the water gives them the expertise required to help a company research and develop products. So these companies rely heavily on the pro staffs for advice on creating new lures, rods, reels, and boats. Even the creation of the simplest gear, such as a pair of fishing pliers, has been influenced by the on-the-water trials of the bass pros.

Since they must make their living casting for cash, the bass pros also are adept at finding the right lure and targeting the best structure and cover to consistently catch enough bass to finish in the money. Weekend anglers might spend some time working the same cover or structure with their confidence lures and a few new ones they think will work. They might catch a few fish, but they usually miss out on the mother lode sitting on that spot.

On the other hand, the tournament pros know how to quickly sort through their myriad of lure boxes and pick the one or two best options that will boat a quick limit. By analyzing the season, weather, water clarity, and available forage, the pros can pinpoint the best presentation for every type of cover and structure without wasting time mulling through their vast array of tackle.

Their expertise and influence on the sport make the touring bass pros the logical choices as my sources for this book. The tips they share in the ensuing chapters should help you find largemouth bass quicker and trigger more strikes whether you are a competitive or recreational angler.

CHAPTER 1

Rods, Reels, and Line

1

Picking a Baitcast Reel

Bass anglers wanting to master various tactics of the pros must make the baitcast reel one of their key tools of the trade. Since reel manufacturers have made baitcasters highly specialized, the choices become more difficult when buying a new reel.

"You want to buy the best quality reel you can afford because it pays off for you in longevity," says bass fishing superstar Kevin VanDam. "It's going to cast better and perform better for you the whole life of the reel."

Gear ratio is a key consideration when buying a new bait-cast reel. VanDam recommends buying a reel with a lower gear ratio, such as 5.3:1, for fishing with crankbaits and a medium gear ratio model (6.2:1 to 6.6:1) for spinnerbaits. A high-speed reel (7.3:1) is VanDam's choice for burning spinnerbaits and square-bill crankbaits. The high-speed reel also allows VanDam to pick up slack line quickly when he is lifting and dropping plastic worms and jigs or popping a topwater lure.

Baitcast buyers should also consider the reel's spool size. VanDam suggests small spool reels are easier to control while casting and backlash less than larger spools. The Michigan

Kevin VanDam recommends using a premium baitcast reel because it will perform better and last longer than cheaper models.

pro prefers small spools for skipping lures under docks and for light-line tactics. However, he opts for larger spools whenever he needs more line capacity for casting large crankbaits long distances or for heavier test lines and braid.

Ball bearings play a key role in keeping the reel tight at all of its pivot points, so the buyer should pay close attention to the quality and quantity of the bearings. "Most of the premium reels have ten ball bearings," says VanDam. "A four ball-bearing reel might feel good at the store, but after a year of use it will probably be done. Those premium reels will feel the same at the end of the season as they did at the beginning."

2

Spinning Reel Options

Baitcast reels execute most bass fishing tactics well, but when touring pros face heavy fishing pressure, they depend on spinning reels to perform finesse techniques on finicky bass.

BASS pro Tim Horton favors spinning reels for drop-shot rigs, shaky head jigs, and small jerk baits. For most of these tactics, Horton spools his spinning reel with 6- or 8-pound test fluorocarbon, which he notes is stronger than 8-pound monofilament and has more sensitivity. The Alabama angler also fills some of his spinning reels with 15-pound braid.

Size counts when selecting a spinning reel for bass fishing. "You don't want to get a micro spinning reel," says Horton, who recommends bass anglers should look for reels with a size thirty or thirty-five spool. He believes a wider spool holds line tighter during a cast, whereas a narrow spool causes line to balloon out of the reel and creates bird nests.

Gear ratios for spinning reels usually range from 4.8:1 to 6.1:1. Horton suggests buying a reel with a gear ratio of at least 5.4:1 since some finesse tactics, such as drop shotting in depths of twenty feet or more, require reeling in line quickly to catch up with a hooked fish.

Spinning reels need a quality drag system for battling a bass on thin line.

Purchasing a spinning reel with a quality drag system is essential for battling a bass on thin line. "You need that drag to be forgiving," says Horton. Although a spinning reel with a rear drag control allows for easier adjustment while fighting a fish, Horton prefers a reel with forward center drag: the drag is more dependable since the control is closer to the spool.

Horton also suggests checking the number of ball bearings in the reel you intend to buy. "The more ball bearings the better the quality, just like a baitcast reel. So having a reel with eight to ten ball bearings is important."

3

Casting Rod Choices

Even though he excels with any rod he picks up, bass-fishing superstar Kevin VanDam relies on certain rod lengths and actions whenever he applies a particular technique.

While rod manufacturers continue to offer a variety of rods for special tactics, there are some models that still handle multiple tasks. VanDam's multipurpose rod is a 6-foot, 10-inch high-modulus spinnerbait model he designed. It allows him to make accurate pitches in tight places but has enough length to cast long distances with topwaters and jerk baits.

Other high-modulus graphite rods VanDam selects for specialized techniques are models measuring six and a half feet and seven feet, two inches. Both models have extra fast tips but plenty of backbone for power lures. The Michigan pro uses a 6 ½-foot medium-heavy action rod for throwing ¼- or ⅜-ounce spinnerbaits in tight places or targets such as thick bushes, laydowns, and boat docks. He prefers the 7-foot, 2-inch medium-heavy rod for burning ¾-ounce spinnerbaits, fishing ledges with ¾- or 1-ounce spinnerbaits, dragging football jigs or Carolina rigs, and working small to mid-size swim baits.

For all of his cranking tactics, VanDam favors rods constructed with a combination of E-glass for limberness and graphite for increased sensitivity. VanDam chooses a 6 ½-foot cranking model with medium action for tossing small topwaters and crankbaits around boat docks and other small targets. He moves up to a 6-foot, 8-inch model with a little stiffer action for casting larger crankbaits.

The most versatile crankbait rods in VanDam's rod box are 7-foot medium and 7-foot medium-heavy models. He favors the 7-foot medium for cranking small to medium diving plugs and relies on the medium-heavy action for running lipless crankbaits through grass.

Two other cranking rods VanDam chooses are a 7-foot, 4-inch version for mid-size crankbaits and a 7-foot, 10-inch model for cranking large deep divers along ledges in the summertime.

Kevin VanDam relies on rods in different actions and lengths for the various tactics he uses on the tournament trail.

4

Spinning Rod Considerations

In the early days of bass fishing, a spinning rod was dubbed a "sissy stick" because its flimsy blank was no match for a heavyweight bass. However, today's spinning rods for bass fishing have stronger backbones to deliver better hook-setting power and to outmuscle hard-running bass. The rods still have a flimsy enough tip, though, for casting or skipping the lightweight lures the pros depend on for finesse tactics.

Length should be a major consideration when choosing the ideal spinning rod for bass fishing. "I like long rods when it comes to baitcast rods but I don't for spinning rods," says Bassmaster pro Tim Horton. "It is more of a control thing for me, so I like a 6-foot, 6-inch to 7-foot spinning rod regardless of the technique I use. I am using light line, so usually it is pretty easy to get a long cast anyway, but I lose control [of the cast] with a longer spinning rod." Horton relies on a seven footer for situations in which he has to make longer casts, but he picks a 6-foot, 6-inch medium-heavy action spinning rod for most of his finesse tactics, including drop shotting, shaky head fishing, and skipping a floating worm. When running a small crankbait in shallow water, Horton opts for the same length rod in a medium action.

Tim Horton favors a 6 ½-foot medium-heavy action spinning rod for most of his finesse techniques.

Horton suggests testing a rod at the store to determine if it has the right amount of stiffness for bass fishing applications. "Put the tip against the floor and put a little bit of pressure on it to see how much bend there is to the tip," Horton says. "I like for it to bend about a quarter of the way down the rod. That is where I like the stiffness of the rod to start. I don't want only the last 10 percent of the rod to bend."

5

Pros' Rod and Reel Combos

Look inside the boat of most touring pros and you'll see a wide array of rod and reel combinations that these elite anglers depend on to catch bass throughout the country. Since they fish a variety of waters on the tournament circuit, the pros need certain rods and reels to deliver maximum performance for specific tactics.

Here are the combos the experts use for the following specialized lures and techniques:

- Shaky heads: Finesse fishing expert Jeff Kriet favors a 3000 series spinning reel and a 7-foot medium-heavy rod with a soft tip but plenty of backbone.
- Dragging football jigs: Arkansas pro Mike McClelland employs a 7-foot, 4-inch medium-heavy rod to make longer casts and move a lot of line on the hookset. He employs either a 6.3:1 gear ratio baitcast reel for fishing depths less than twenty feet or a 7.0:1 model for fishing deeper.
- Waking spinnerbaits: A medium-heavy 7-foot or 7-foot, 3-inch rod with a soft tip works best when McClelland burns a spinnerbait. A 7.0:1 baitcaster makes it easier for him to keep the spinnerbait waking.

- Flipping: When Denny Brauer wants to punch through thick stuff, he selects a stiff 7-foot, 7-inch flipping stick. The Texas pro employs a reel he designed for flipping that handles 60-pound braid and has a strong drag system for winching fish out of heavy cover.
- Deep cranking: Long casts are essential for cranking specialist Paul Elias, so he chooses a 7-foot, 11-inch graphite rod. His favorite cranking reel features a 4.8:1 gear ratio for the power to wind in these hard-driving lures.
- Swimbaits: Oklahoman Fred Roumbanis likes to cover a lot of water with his swimbaits, so he makes long casts

with a 7-foot, 4-inch or 7-foot, 6-inch medium or medium-heavy rod and selects a high speed reel (6.3:1 gear ratio) to catch up with bass that usually inhale his lure and swim at him.

Fred Roumbanis prefers a medium or medium-heavy rod and high-speed reel for his swimbait presentations.

6

Monofilament or Fluorocarbon?

There are lines available today for nearly every situation a bass angler will encounter. Anglers now have the option of trying monofilament, fluorocarbon, or braid, so they have to decide which type of line is best for their style of fishing.

"I have found uses for all the lines and I think it has helped me be a better all-around fisherman when I use the right line for the right situation," says Bassmaster Elite Series pro Kenyon Hill.

The Oklahoma angler's choice for the best multipurpose line is monofilament. "It has been an all-around great fishing line for years," he says. "It does a great job and it is affordable."

Since fluorocarbon's stiffness makes it tough to spool on a spinning reel, Hill combines a super line and fluorocarbon for his spinning gear. He usually fills his reel with 14-pound Fire-Line and employs a double uni-knot to attach a 10- to 12-foot leader of fluorocarbon ranging from 6- to 20-pound test. He trims the tag ends of the lines as close as possible to the knot and then bonds the knot tighter with a drop of superglue.

The sensitivity of fluorocarbon makes it Hill's first choice whenever he uses lures that require plenty of feel, such as worms, jigs, and Carolina-rigged baits. "Braid is also sensitive, but I feel I get more bites on a line that is more transparent (fluorocarbon) as opposed to the braided line, especially when it comes to a finesse bait in which a fish can come up and examine it," Hill says.

Hill prefers monofilament when he uses suspending jerk baits because fluorocarbon tends to sink, which affects the buoyancy of his lures. However, he switches back to fluorocarbon for running deep-diving crankbaits, because the line's ability to sink increases the depth of his lures and its low-stretch qualities improve chances for a better hookup.

Kenyon Hill relies on fluorocarbon line when throwing deep-diving crankbaits to increase the lure's running depth and improve his hook-setting percentages.

7

Applications for Braided Line

BASS winner Kenyon Hill opts for braided line for deep cranking in heavy cover on big-bass lakes, such as Amistad or Falcon in Texas. "A 20-pound test braided line has a very small diameter (6- or 8-pound test) so it will dive very well, and then you can put the power to lean on those bad boys to get them out of that heavy stuff," he says.

Braided line is also Hill's choice for reaction-type lures such as spinnerbaits or lipless crankbaits and a variety of topwater lures (surface plugs, buzz baits, and plastic frogs). Although he can cast his topwater lures farther with mono-filament, Hill favors throwing surface lures with braided line because it floats well and has better hook-setting power because of its low stretch.

Braided line's low stretch also comes in handy when Hill fishes spinnerbaits and lipless crankbaits through milfoil and hydrilla beds. He can rip these lures through the weeds easier with braided line, which triggers more strikes. However, if he is fishing worms or jigs in the grass, Hill opts for fluorocarbon for the sensitivity and low-visibility qualities of the line.

Hill notices some braided line will last all year on a reel, but it should be replaced when it starts to fade and fray.

Braided line is ideal for topwater plugs, because it floats well and its low stretch provides better hook-setting power.

Frequently fishing in cold or dirty water causes Hill to change all of his line more often. "If your line starts getting dirty and tacky, it doesn't come off the spool as well," he says. Old and dirty line that sticks to the spool results in more bird nests and backlashes.

Pros rely on various rods, reels, and lines to apply a wide range of techniques on the tournament trail.

CHAPTER 2

Defining Structure and Types

8

Get the Drop on Bass

Top pro Aaron Martens frequently looks for sudden changes in the bottom contour of a lake because he knows these drops attract bass year-round.

"Normally a drop-off is a good place for the bass to feed and it concentrates the fish," says Martens. "If you have a big flat, it is hard to locate the fish on it, but if you have a big flat with a drop-off on it, about 75 percent of the fish will be on the drop-off most of the time."

Productive drop-offs can be as extreme as a bluff wall with a ledge that drops down to 100 feet or as subtle as a 1-foot deep ditch. "The subtlest depression on a flat can make all the difference in the world," says Martens. The Bassmaster Elite Series star notes a drop is a key hangout for bass because it allows the fish to rapidly move up to shallow water when conditions are ideal for feeding and also allows quick access to deeper water if the fish need to retreat after the passage of a cold front.

The Alabama pro targets drops along creek channel swings in the early spring when pre-spawn bass are migrating to the spawning banks and in late fall when baitfish and bass move back out of the creeks. He prefers main channel drop-offs during summer, winter, and early fall.

Aaron Martens finds large concentrations of bass nearly year-round along drop-offs.

9

Ledges for Summertime Fun

Many bass leave the bank for the wide-open spaces of the lake during the summer. Finding them was easy when the fish were close to shore, but now it becomes more of a challenge.

While the novice angler continues to pound the shoreline and catch small bass, Kentucky pro Mark Menendez targets offshore structure that produces for him throughout the summer. Once hot weather arrives, Menendez locates bass along ledges, a structure with many of the same features (lay-downs, stump rows, brush, and rock piles) anglers find along the bank.

Similar to steps in a swimming pool, ledges serve as stairways for bass. "A ledge is just a shallow area with immediate deep-water access that provides a congregation point and/or a feeding area," says Menendez.

"The structure itself can be anything—a point, river channel, swing, bluff bank, or a flat that has immediate juncture to deep water."

While some anglers can trick ledge bass with shallow-water tactics, Menendez relies on two techniques for probing the drops. His favorite methods for catching bass along ledges are cranking a deep-diving crankbait and stroking a jig.

Mark Menendez starts fishing ledges first with a deep-diving crankbait to catch the most aggressive bass first.

Deep cranking can produce a limit in a hurry, so Menendez prepares for this quick action by having five rods with crankbaits ready on the front deck. "Once you find the sweet spot, you're ready to start catching them on every throw," says Menendez who frequently takes five bass on five casts.

As the sun gets higher and the fish become less aggressive, Menendez switches to the jig-stroking technique. "The stroking aspect of ledge fishing is getting a reaction strike from relatively deep-water fish (in the 10- to 20-foot range)," advises Menendez. This technique involves jerking a jig along the top of the ledge all the way to the drop.

10

Pinpointing Bass on Ledges

When touring pros venture offshore, they do a lot more screen-watching than the novice angler does to find and catch bass.

"We don't cast until we see the fish," says Alabama pro Tim Horton. "It can really take a lot of time and effort to get on ledges and learn what to look for."

Reading the map in his GPS/depth finder and having confidence in his ability to distinguish what type of fish he sees on his graph are Horton's keys to fishing ledges.

"White bass and stripers are usually off the bottom and there will be a lot of them on the screen," he advises. "There are always a lot more schools of those fish than the bass and they will be tighter together. A school of white bass will come all the way up to within a few feet of the surface. Bass will stay down on the bottom and are going to do what I call 'sitting up on the table.' That's when you can really catch them—when they are sitting right up on top of the ledge. Then you will usually see ten to fifteen bumps right on the bottom."

Ledges on power-generation reservoirs are Horton's favorite summertime offshore targets. "The number one thing I look for when I go to those lakes is water clarity, because that is going to tell me how deep the baitfish are," he says. Horton notes that, on stained water reservoirs, the fish will hold on ledges only eight to twelve feet deep, but bass on clearer impoundments will gather on 15- to 20-foot ledges.

Finding the sweet spot of a ledge with his depth finder is crucial to Horton's offshore structure strategy. "I will figure-eight a spot sometimes six or seven times until I see where the fish are locating," he says.

Before he starts fishing a ledge, Tim Horton thoroughly scouts the structure with his side-imaging unit.

11

Score Big on Humps

Visit just about any bait-and-tackle shop near a reservoir and you'll hear the tale of the local angler who pulled up on one spot and caught 100 bass.

"It doesn't happen real often but it happens," former Bassmaster Classic champion Alton Jones says of these extraordinary catches. "Almost always when you hear that type of a situation, they're talking about fishing a hump."

The Texas pro considers humps any type of irregular bottom feature that gives bass a place to rely on predatory instincts. "Bass are the classic predators," he says. "They like to sit in a spot that gives them a definite advantage over whatever they are trying to eat. A hump certainly does that." Jones notes that humps also have deep-water access nearby, which allows the fish to take a quick escape route when necessary.

"Some humps are better than others," says Jones. "The best humps are always the ones located near some sort of underwater pathway like a creek channel or a weed line—something that the bass can follow from shallow to deep water."

In the feeder creeks of reservoirs, Jones looks for high spots in the channel where the bottom rises from fifteen feet to eight feet deep. "That's going to be one of those places where you might pull up and find giant schools of bass," he advises.

Some humps produce bass year-round, but Jones usually keys on this structure from the post-spawn through fall. He rates summer as the prime time and spring as the least productive season for fishing humps.

Jones probes a hump with a subtle presentation first, so he starts with a crankbait and follows up with a Carolina

rig. "The big fish are going to be the spookiest, so if I start throwing my Carolina rig out there, the first fish I am going to spook off is that giant," says Jones.

Offshore humps produce quality bass for Alton Jones during the post-spawn of late spring and throughout the summer.

12

Bluff Points for Winter Bass

A point at the end of a bluff line attracts bass during the winter, because it allows bass quick access to both deep and shallow water. "Those fish aren't going to be way up on a flat like they are when they spawn or after they spawn or the

Bass move up to the shallowest part of a bluff point on sunny, breezy winter days.

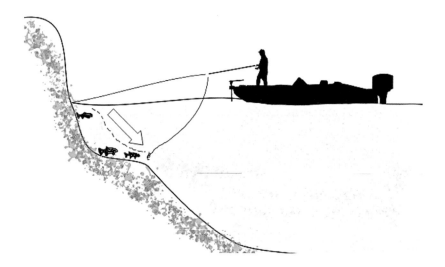

summertime," says North Carolina touring pro David Fritts. "They are going to be close to deep water where they can move easily up and down."

The weather determines where bass will position on a bluff point. "The fish will be right on the bank along the point if the sun is shining and the wind is blowing, but if it is cold the fish will be on the end of the point," says Fritts. The FLW competitor notes these main lake fish will stay on the bluff points in the spring until the water temperature starts to climb close to the 60-degree mark, then those pre-spawn bass start moving into the spawning coves and pockets.

Fan casting a crankbait around the bluff point produces wintertime bass for Fritts. He positions his boat over a depth of twenty to twenty-five feet and tries to run his crankbait from the shallows of the point down to fifteen to eighteen feet deep.

13

Points for Post-spawn Bass

When late spring turns into early summer, the waiting line can get pretty long on some of the most popular points of your favorite reservoir.

"Most of the fish are through spawning and they start pulling out to the points and moving out to the drops," says Bassmaster Elite Series pro Jeff Kriet.

FLW Tour pro Dan Morehead believes points are good rest areas for bass in transition during this time. "There are a lot of fish migrating," he says. "A few are still spawning but most are leaving, and points just make a good stopping off area for migrating fish."

Sometimes Kriet will fish the whole point, but on most occasions he idles over the structure and keeps a constant vigil on his electronics. The Oklahoma pro looks for the steepest drop on the point because he knows the fish stack up on this spot during late spring and early summer. He pores over the whole point in search of the sweet spot because many times the steepest drop on a point is along its sides rather than on the end. These spots also usually contain the most bottom irregularities, such as bigger rocks or debris that has been swept in by current over the years.

Morehead usually targets long, sloping gravel points towards the backs of the spawning bays in late spring. On some points he targets sweet spots such as a solitary stump or a rock change along the bottom, but on other points he prefers fishing the whole structure.

The Kentucky pro will also spend some time on his electronics when idling along a point, but he is mainly looking for balls of baitfish. He believes finding baitfish on the points is a key during this time of year because bass need to hang around plenty of food after enduring the rigors of spawning.

BASS pro Jeff Kriet keys on points after bass finish spawning and start migrating to deeper water.

14

Channel Swinging

Bends in the old river and creek channels of an impoundment are prime staging spots for bass, especially in the spring and fall. The fish use these bends or channel swings as resting stops before moving into coves or pockets for the spawn or annual fall migration, and they will revisit these spots on their way out of the shallows during the post-spawn and late fall.

FLW pro David Fritts looks for channel swings whenever he fishes highland reservoirs. He knows channel bends on these impoundments provide a spot where bass can move up quickly into the shallows to feed and then drop back down into deeper water when the weather changes or the lake level starts dropping. "The best channel swings that I have ever fished are the ones that I don't see with my naked eye," says Fritts who relies on his electronics to find the ideal channel swing. "I go out there and find where a creek channel makes a turn, and it might be fifteen feet on top of it and then it falls out forty feet deep. It takes a little bit longer to find those but that is what I like to look for."

Some channels have long bends, so Fritts recommends finding "something different" along the bend to pinpoint bass. "I like a channel swing that actually hits close to the bank and then comes back out with a two-stage step, with one step that goes down to twelve to fifteen feet deep and then the next step is straight off [into the channel]." Any dips in the channel created by current scouring the bottom are also sweet spots on channel swings.

Fritts's favorite tactic for channel swings is to position his boat parallel to the bend and run a crankbait along the drop-off to keep his lure in the strike zone throughout his presentation.

A crankbait is David Fritts's favorite lure for probing channel swings.

15

Dissecting Flats

Vast expanses of shallow-water areas seem to sprawl endlessly on many lakes throughout the country. These sprawling shallow flats can be found on natural lakes, man-made reservoirs, or rivers and are bass magnets despite their unattractive looks.

Finding bass on these long stretches of shallow structure can be an intimidating test for the novice angler; however, touring pros know how to dissect a flat to separate the dead water from the sweet spots. Bassmaster Elite Series pro Pete Ponds knows flats are migration routes for bass to spawn in the spring and feed in the fall. The Mississippi angler often relies on water temperature to pinpoint how shallow bass will be holding in these seasons and what lures he should throw along the flats.

Whenever he encounters a large area of continuous shallow water, Ponds tracks down bass in a hurry by looking for key targets including stump rows, ditches, fencerows, roadbeds, and break lines.

One of Pond's favorite spots to find bass along a flat is any indentation in the bottom contour. "The slightest variance will make a big difference," says Ponds. An example is a spot that drops to six feet deep while the surrounding area has a depth of four feet.

When the water temperature reaches 55 to 57 degrees in the spring, Ponds looks for bass on any cover along the edges of the flats. As the water temperature climbs to 62 to 63 degrees, bigger bass move up into the indentations on the flats to spawn.

During the spawn, Ponds avoids shady spots along the flats and keys on the areas receiving the most sunshine. "Bass have to have sun to warm up and hatch their eggs," says Ponds.

Any gravel bottom or mussel shell beds are prime areas along flats for spawning bass. "Any type of hard surface is better than a mud bottom along a flat in the springtime," Ponds says.

Mississippi pro Pete Ponds looks for stump rows to pinpoint bass along vast stretches of flats.

16

Boat Ramp Hotspots

Tournament veteran George Cochran has been known to go to extremes to find bass, either making long runs to remote spots or staying right where he launches his boat.

"A boat ramp is completely different than anything in the lake," discloses Cochran. "Most people take them for granted but I have caught so many bass around ramps."

No matter what body of water he fishes, Cochran checks out boat ramps because he knows the man-made structure is a bass magnet. "What is so perfect about it is it starts on the bank and runs zero to twenty feet out depending on the lake," describes Cochran. "There is also always rock and gravel around it and riprap within fifty yards of it to keep the bank from washing out."

"Bass key in on ramps just about any time of the year," Cochran reveals. Many boat ramps are constructed on points or tapering banks, which makes the spots ideal for both migrating and stationary bass.

All boat ramps have three main targets to fish: the two sides of the concrete ramp and the deep end of the concrete slab. "You need to fish it just like you would a boat dock," suggests Cochran. "What I always try to do is fish out on the deep side the first cast or two. If I catch one out there, there is usually a school and I will catch several. But if you throw shallow up on the ramp and catch a fish there first and drag it through the prime area of the ramp you might disturb the school and only catch that one fish." If the outside edges fail to produce any fish, then Cochran starts easing up on the ramp to target shallower fish.

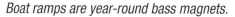
Boat ramps are year-round bass magnets.

17

Tailrace Tactics

Watching the river flow is all Bassmaster pro Russ Lane needs to do to determine if a tailrace will produce for him.

"You don't have to count on the sun shining for you or the clouds coming in or none of that stuff," says Lane. "Current forces bass to do what they are going to do, and for the most part they are going to hide behind current breaks."

The velocity of the current determines whether Lane fishes close to the dam or farther downstream. "You just want to get in a situation where the current is fast enough that it can place the fish behind different objects without pushing them completely into a backwater area or something," says Lane.

The Alabama pro watches how his lures (usually a 1-ounce spinnerbait or a 1-ounce football jig and craw) react to the water flow to tell if the current is suitable enough for his presentation. "I try to keep my bait in contact with the bottom, and if I am not able to keep it there through experimenting with weight and line size, then I probably need to go back down river a little bit to find a softer current," he says.

Once he finds the right current speed, Lane surveys the area for any obstructions that change the current's course. A visible current break that Lane keys on sometimes is a big slick lay-down log that has lost all of its branches. "For some reason the fish sit behind those better than other wood," discloses Lane.

Concrete slabs for power lines that run across the river also attract bass seeking shelter from the current. Any rocks jutting out from the bank also breaks the current, but Lane's favorite current breaks in tailraces are underwater rocks that he finds with his electronics.

Heavy lures, such as a 1-ounce football jig, are necessary for catching bass in the current of tailraces.

The seasons dictate the type of structure bass prefer throughout the year.

CHAPTER 3

Defining Cover

18

Rock On for Bass

Rock banks are ideal year-round hangouts for bass since this type of cover radiates heat during the colder months, attracts baitfish feeding on algae in the warmer months, and provides a hard bottom for bass to build nests during the spawn. Bass prefer boulder-size rocks in the wintertime and then opt for chunk rock banks in the spring, summer, and fall to feed on crawfish and baitfish. Pea gravel is usually the preferred type of bottom for spawning bass in rocky lakes.

Touring pro Dave Wolak bases his lure choice for rock banks on the forage bass are targeting at the time. "One of the main forages on a rocky bank is a crawfish, so I am looking for something that I can kind of climb and crawl along the rocks," says Wolak.

In cold-water situations, the North Carolina pro's pick for imitating a crawfish is a ⅜- or ½-ounce football jig tipped with a soft plastic craw. Wolak opts for the football-shaped jig over a conventional style jig because he can work it along the rocky bottom easier. "The wider head profile doesn't get caught in the rocks as much," he claims.

During the shad spawn in the spring, Wolak knows bass are keying on baitfish then, so he moves to the shallows and knocks the rocks with a square-bill crankbait. He reels the lure at a fast clip to make the crankbait deflect off the rocks and trigger a reaction strike.

Summertime bass on the rocks are also feeding on shad, but Wolak tempts these fish with a jerk bait. The tournament veteran favors this lure because it allows him to cover water quickly, and he can aggressively pop the lure to imitate the fleeing baitfish in the area.

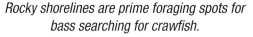

Rocky shorelines are prime foraging spots for bass searching for crawfish.

19

Single Rocks for More Bass

Rocks can be found everywhere, especially on a highland reservoir or natural lake, so Texas pro Alton Jones looks for an isolated rock or pile of rocks of a certain size to find concentrations of bass. "It depends on the situation, but in most cases I would like to have [a single rock] the size of a sofa or a pile of smaller rocks about that size," he says.

"Rocks do so many things," says Jones. "When there is rock there is usually a break line, and a lot of times the rock itself is a break line. A rock can also be a good current break."

The mood of the fish dictates which lures Jones works around solitary rocks. He usually starts with a crankbait to pick off the most aggressive fish and then moves in tighter to the cover and pitches soft plastics, such as a stick worm, to mop up on the rest of the bass schooling around the rock.

Isolated rocks (or just about any isolated cover) usually identify a bass' kitchen, according to Jones. "Even if you make a trip there and don't catch fish, at some point during the day there is probably going to be a school of bass that uses it," he says. So make sure you make a return trip or two to that bass' chow line throughout the day.

When keying on submerged isolated rocks or rock piles, Jones relies heavily on his electronics with the side-imaging feature. Once he pinpoints rocks with his electronics, Jones will throw out a marker buoy about fifteen feet to the side of the cover. "It helps to put a buoy out at first to give myself a visual frame of reference," he says. After making multiple casts to the cover, Jones removes the buoy to avoid drawing the attention of any onlookers.

Solitary rocks have many features that are appealing to schools of bass.

20

Bald Spots for Weed Bass

Thick weeds usually attract several bass seeking the shade and shelter of this type of cover, but there are times when the pros target sparse weed growth. Bald is beautiful to professional bass angler Kelly Jordon whenever he fishes grass lines on reservoirs during the spring.

When a reservoir's water level is drawn down in the winter, aquatic vegetation on any shallow high spot, such as a point, underwater ridge, or hump, dies off as it becomes exposed to dry land. Spring rains usually raise the lake level two to ten feet and bald spots in the grass lines form where the dry high spots become inundated with water again. Jordon

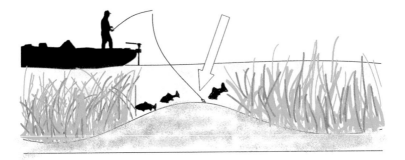

Bald spots in weeds are staging areas for pre-spawn bass before the fish make a move to the spawning banks.

targets these bald spots because he knows these are staging areas where pre-spawn bass hold before the fish move to the flooded bushes or willows along the shoreline.

"Anytime you find a bald spot, the more isolated it is, the better it is," says Jordon. "You can hit the gravy train if you can find a little high spot like that."

Jordan relies on two presentations to hit the prime areas of bald spots. "A Carolina rig and a crankbait are easiest to use because they help you feel the bottom of the bald spot," he says "Once you find that bald spot, you can make repeated casts to the same area with other lures (spinnerbaits, soft plastic jerk baits, and suspending stick baits) as well."

21

Weeding Out Fall Bass

Weeds are wonderful spots to search for bass when the water is warm, but some anglers shy away from this type of cover during autumn when leaves on the trees and aquatic vegetation start turning brown.

Weeds dying in the fall causes oxygen depletion in some areas that can lead to poor fishing, but Bassmaster Elite Series pro Tim Horton knows some dead vegetation can be just as good as the green stuff. "Some of the backwater areas when the weeds are dying will have some pH problems, but out on the main lake where there is current, that will not be an issue," says Horton, who concentrates on fishing weeds until the water temperature falls into the low fifties. "The fish will tend to go the weeds in the backs of creeks in the fall, but if there is good ample cover on the main lake, you can still catch them there."

Autumn's cooler weather allows bass to roam freely through the weeds at all depths. "That is one of the unique things about the fall: You can catch fish from the surface to ten feet deep in the vegetation," says Horton. "The temperature starts to get the same throughout the water column, and I vary the depth by the day and location that I am fishing. The fish will get a little higher up in the weeds in the fall with the cooler water."

A ½-ounce buzz bait becomes Horton's primary lure for coaxing these suspended bass from the weeds. "A topwater bait can really be dynamite too in the fall on the outside edges of the grass," says Horton. Whenever he sees a lot of surface activity in the vegetation, Horton will buzz a hollow-bodied frog across the top of the weeds. Other lures he tosses to the weeds in the fall include spinnerbaits, jigs, and lipless crankbaits.

Tim Horton coaxes bites from suspended bass in the weeds with a buzz bait during the fall.

Standing Timber Tricks

Touring pro Stacey King has plenty of experience fishing wood cover on his home waters of Table Rock and Missouri's Truman Reservoir, so he knows what bass like when the fish seek refuge in the trees.

"My favorite lure for fishing timber is a jig," says King. The Missouri pro favors throwing a jig in the timber because it produces bass year-round, except during the spawn when the fish leave the trees.

The depth of the fish determines the weight of the jig King selects. "You have to determine first whether they are suspended or on the bottom," he says. When the fish are suspended, he will use a lighter jig (⅜-ounce), but he will switch to a ¾-ounce model when bass are hugging the bottom.

"Sometimes a finesse jig is good (clear-water and winter situations) and sometimes a bulkier big jig is good," says King. "If the bite is really good I like a big jig (¾-ounce) with a big plastic chunk on it."

The type of trees he targets also dictates which jig King picks. When fishing around pole timber, King opts for a football jig for bumping into the tree trunks, but if he wants to slide his lure through the thick branches of cedar trees, the tournament veteran prefers a jig with a pointed nose to mini-mize hang-ups.

Other lures King likes to throw around timber include topwater plugs such as a Zara Spook, spinnerbaits, and Texas-rigged creature baits. He favors throwing the topwater lures around the timber in spring and fall when the fish are suspended in the tops of cedars and oak trees.

Running a ⅜- or ½-ounce double willowleaf spinnerbait through the trees also produces for King in autumn. "When there is a cloudy, windy day, those big fish will come up around the tops of those trees and I will wake those spinner-baits besides the trees then," he says.

Bumping a jig into the wood produces bass year-round on reservoirs filled with standing timber.

23

Visualizing Laydowns

A tree blown down into the water offers bass one of the best pieces of cover in the shallows. Commonly referred to as a laydown, a downed tree provides plenty of hiding spots for bass with its multiple branches and large trunk.

"What really intrigues me about laydowns is what you can't see underneath the water," says Arkansas pro Stephen Browning. "You have to use your visualization of what you think is lying down there and how that particular piece of cover looks below the water. I will look at the other trees standing on the bank that are the same diameter and try to figure out about how far out the tip of that tree might be. So many people want to fire to what they can see and lots of times they miss a fish's house because they are fishing exactly what everybody else is fishing."

The Bassmaster pro keys on laydowns along gradual sloping banks close to a bottom contour change, such as a creek channel or ditch. When he finds an ideal laydown, Browning fishes the outside edges of the tree first to catch the most aggressive bass and then works his way into the trunk. "You don't want to catch one out of the middle of the tree and spook the rest of the fish in there," he warns.

52

Work the outside edge of a laydown first to catch the most aggressive bass and avoid spooking the rest of the fish in the cover.

24

Stump Bumping a Crankbait

When bass move up out of the river and creek channels to feed, one of their favorite ambush points is a stump. This type of wood cover usually contains a washed-out gnarly root system that bass can hide in while waiting for baitfish to wander into their strike zone.

Since the flats next to river and creek channels are usually lined with numerous rows of stumps, you will need a lure that covers water quickly and avoids tangling in the roots. Bassmaster Elite Series pro Kevin Short likes to bump the stumps with a crankbait, so he wants a lure that can bang off the cover without hanging and also take the constant abuse of hitting solid wood. When the water temperature ranges from 60 to 100 degrees, he selects a square-bill balsa crankbait. "It deflects really well," he says. "I think you could throw it at a chicken wire fence and it would come through without getting hung up."

The Arkansas pro usually makes short pitches (twenty-five to thirty feet) around stumps in dirty water but will make longer casts to the wood cover if he is fishing clearer water. Short cranks his balsa bait at a high speed to bang it off the stumps to trigger reaction strikes. "Sometimes you have to bounce it off the stump multiple times," says Short. "Sometimes you might have to bounce that bait four or five times off of each side of the stump before you get a bite, particularly if the fish are spawning around the stumps and aren't extremely aggressive."

A high-speed reel is essential for banging the square-bill crankbait into the stumps and making it deflect off the wood, so Short counts on a 6.3:1 baitcast model. He also cranks his lure with heavier abrasion-resistant line (15- to 17-pound fluorocarbon) that can handle the constant rubbing into the stumps.

A square-bill crankbait deflected off the wood triggers strikes from bass hanging around stumps.

Drop Shotting Stumps

When bass begin their fall migration to the shallows, one of their favorite stops along the way is a stump located at the edge of a creek channel.

Since stumps are also popular targets for anglers to hit as they follow bass to the shallows, these transition spots get hammered with spinnerbaits, crankbaits, jigs, and other power baits all day long. Count Mississippi pro Pete Ponds as one of those who likes to flip jigs or bang crankbaits into the stumps, but he changes tactics when he notices the stumps are receiving heavy fishing pressure.

Then the Bassmaster competitor breaks out his spinning tackle and ties on a drop shot rig. "Bass see jigs flipped into those stumps all the time, so this is almost a finesse fishing tactic," says Ponds.

Submerged isolated stumps produce best for this presentation, so the key to finding these targets is a good pair of sunglasses with the right lens tint. Ponds favors yellow lenses for finding the dark spots, but he suggests other colors like amber work as well.

Once he pinpoints his target, Ponds approaches the stump in the same manner as a flipping presentation, keeping the boat about twenty feet or less from the cover and making a short pitch. After the drop shot weight hits bottom, Ponds shakes his bait on a slack line, which prevents the weight from moving away from the stump and pulling the bait out of the strike zone.

After shaking the rig in place for a few seconds, Ponds retrieves the lure and pitches to the other side of the stump. He usually saturates the stump with pitches to all of its sides before moving to the next target.

Pond's drop shot rig consists of a 6-inch straight tail worm attached to a 2/0 hook tied about eight inches above a ¼-ounce elongated weight.

When fishing pressure gets heavy around stump rows, try drop shotting a finesse worm next to the wood cover.

Knocking Docks for Summer Bass

"Bass live around boat docks year-round," says Bass-master competitor Kevin Short. "However, summertime might be the absolute best time to catch those fish because they get so oriented to the shade. Once you figure where they are at on one or two docks, you can catch a fish off of every single dock like that."

The Arkansas pro favors docks that are either isolated, on a point, or near a channel swing. His favorite type of dock is a pier with wooden posts. "The wood typically has a lot of algae on it, which attracts shad and bluegill," says Short. "[Bass] get very specific about where they are at on those docks and that lasts for weeks at a time."

In the morning, Short fishes a jig around docks to catch bass on the bottom, but he switches tactics as the sun rises higher. "As the day goes on, I have seen where those fish come up and suspend higher and higher," he says. "I have actually caught them in the middle of the day on a buzz bait at the end of a dock."

His most productive lure for bass suspended around docks is a square-bill crankbait in shad or bluegill hues. "I look for something swimming around the dock and try to match my bait color to that," he says.

Short makes long casts at different angles to the dock and tries to keep his crankbait as close as possible to the wooden posts. "I take my time going around there and make two to three casts on each post," he says. "On every cast I try to hit a post, two posts, three posts, or however many I can get." If the water is low enough, he makes underhand roll casts to deliver his crankbait into the shade underneath the dock's deck.

When bass seek shade under docks in the summertime, Kevin Short tempts them by knocking crankbaits into the wooden posts of the piers.

27

Fall for Dock Bass

B oat docks become homes for baitfish and bass during their annual fall migration.

"Shad in the fall are up towards the surface, and the boat docks give the shad a lot of cover, and then the bass relate to the boat docks," says Bassmaster pro Edwin Evers. Docks provide a giant canopy that generates plenty of shade extending from deep water to the shallows, thus making it ideal for bass to roam the length of the docks to ambush baitfish.

The Oklahoma pro narrows his search for the most productive docks to the backs of creeks. "Usually that first or second dock in the backs of the creeks is the best," he suggests. Shallow docks near a creek channel swing are also prime spots for bass. Evers also tries docks along secondary points or those sitting in front of banks with rock changes.

The tournament competitor finds bass either suspended under the main part of the dock or in inches of water under the walkway. "A lot of times in the fall the best spots are all in the back, either the back corner or the first float on the walkway or right underneath the walkway where it meets the dock," says Evers.

Bass are easier to pinpoint when they move to the backs of the docks, but it becomes more of a challenge to target the fish when they suspend on the main part of the structure. The fish can be scattered anywhere along the dock and will suspend at different depths depending on the weather, time of day, and water clarity.

When he perceives bass are near the surface, Evers relies on a Heddon Zara Spook that he works at a quick pace. If fish ignore his Spook, Evers switches to fast-moving lures such as a spinnerbait or a crankbait that allows him to cover more water more quickly.

Boat docks provide plenty of ambush points for bass in the fall when the fish are feeding heavily on shad.

28

Target Isolated Flooded Bushes

When a rising lake level inundates the shoreline, bass have miles of flooded bushes to seek shelter, so finding the fish could take countless hours if you try to fish all of the new cover.

Oklahoma pro Edwin Evers keys on solitary bushes because he knows less is better for bass in this situation. "If you have just one flooded bush along that shoreline, that is all that bass has to relate to. It is a lot easier ambush point for that fish because it can see 360 degrees and ambush anything that comes by it," he says.

The BASS angler has caught four or five quality bass on many occasions from a lonely flooded bush. "It is all about the location and how close it is to deep water, especially if it is the only one on a point or the last one in the back of a pocket," says Evers. He believes the best isolated bushes are usually fifty to 100 feet or more apart from the rest of the flooded cover.

A productive solitary bush can also be in ultra shallow water. "Bass don't have to stand on their heads so [the bush] doesn't have to be very deep," says Evers, who has caught bass from lone bushes in ten inches to one foot of water.

Once he catches bass from a couple of isolated bushes, Evers spends the rest of his day making a milk run to more lone bushes.

Two of Evers's favorite presentations for isolated bushes are hopping a jig off the bottom or swimming it around and through the bush. For swimming a jig or hopping it in stained water, Evers prefers slower falling ¼- or ⅜-ounce models. He switches to a ½- or ¾-ounce jig to create a faster fall and trigger a reaction strike in clearer water.

Edwin Evers looks for a solitary flooded bush to catch bass in the shallows when a lake level rises and inundates miles of shoreline bushes.

Brush Up for Post-spawn Bass

The rigors of spawning are over and now it's time for bass to find a good place to recuperate.

On lakes devoid of natural cover, manmade brush piles are the prime place for bass to rest before migrating to deep water. A brush pile provides cover and shade and draws bait-fish that feed on its algae-covered limbs—all the essentials post-spawn bass require for their recovery process. "When the fish get done spawning, they hole up in those brush piles from six to ten feet deep and recuperate before they move back out on the ledges," says Mark Tucker, a Bassmaster Open winner.

The Missouri pro targets points that are adjacent to spawning flats in order to pinpoint post-spawn bass. Time of day dictates which lure Tucker selects for probing the brush pile. "The biggest thing is to figure out how the fish are positioned in the brush pile," says Tucker. "A lot of times early in the morning, the fish will get up on top of it and hit the lure on the initial fall. Very seldom will you have to work it through the brush. When the sun gets up, you will have to sink it a little more and work a jig up and down to get the bite."

A straight-tail worm attached to a ⅛-ounce jighead is Tucker's choice for post-spawn bass suspended above the brush. "Eighty percent of the time, the fish hit it on the initial fall," he says. If the fish fail to nab it on the descent, Tucker lets the worm fall to the bottom and shakes it three times before reeling it in for another cast.

For bass holding tight to the cover, Tucker opts for a ¼- or ⁵⁄₁₆-ounce jig and plastic chunk or craw. Another brush pile option for Tucker is a Texas-rigged creature bait with a 4/0 sproat hook and ⁵⁄₁₆-ounce sinker.

Post-spawn bass hanging around brush piles will suspend above the brush early in the morning and move down closer to the cover as the sun gets brighter.

30

Drop Shotting Brush Piles

When the water temperature climbs into the bath water range, FLW pro Brett Hite goes light with his line and lures to catch lazy summertime bass. He opts for a 5-inch stick worm or a 6-inch finesse worm.

The touring pro sets up the worm on a drop shot rig with a $3/16$- or $1/4$-ounce cylindrical weight, which he believes hangs up less when working it through brush. Hite varies the length of his 7-pound fluorocarbon line between his hook and sinker depending on if the fish are suspended or hugging the bottom. "The length of a Plano (utility) box is a good reference point for starting the length of your drop," says Hite. "If I think the fish might be eating crawdads, I will go to a little bit shorter drop; but if I think they are up off the bottom, I will go to a longer leader."

The Arizona angler searches for brush piles along main lake points or islands with steep breaks. He keys on the 15- to 40-foot range where most of the fish will be within eight feet of the bottom.

When he locates the fish on the depth finder, Hite tries either a vertical or horizontal presentation. For his vertical presentation, Hite lets the rig fall to the depth of the shadow of the brush showing on his locator. After letting the drop shot sit for ten to thirty seconds, he shakes the rig and then lets the worm settle again. If this fails to trigger a strike, Hite lifts the rig until he feels it hit part of the brush and then shakes it again.

When drop-shotting horizontally, Hite casts out his rig and lets it fall to the bottom. "I drag it and lift it over the cover and let it fall. After it settles I pick up to see if any pressure is there."

Brett Hite puts a finesse worm on a drop shot rig to catch bass suspended over brush piles in the summertime.

Any type of wood cover, such as flooded bushes, logs, stumps, or standing timber, serves as an excellent hideout and ambush point for bass.

CHAPTER 4

Seasonal Movements

31

Transition Banks for
Pre-spawn Bass

When bass get that urge to reproduce in the spring, they make an annual trek along a traditional migration route. The migration routes in manmade reservoirs throughout most of the country are usually creek and river channels that allow the fish to move from deep-water winter sanctuaries to the shallow spawning flats. The key to finding pre-spawn bass is to locate transition banks, which serve as holding areas along the migration route.

"I am always looking for a bay where bass spawn," says former Bassmaster Classic champ Alton Jones. "Then I start backing my way out to find where it transitions and there is some good depth (eight to ten feet)." The Texas pro searches for a stopping point where bass from deep water rest for a while before moving to the spawning flat. In some cases the distance between the deep water and the shallow spawning spot can be a couple of feet or the length of an average cast.

Following a meandering channel into a cove helps BASS pro Brent Chapman find transition banks. "Wherever that channel swings up against the bank is typically a transition and the fish seem to associate with those transitions on up to the spawn," discloses Chapman. "A bass relates to edges and a transition creates an edge of some sort."

The Kansas angler believes edges exist along transitions where the bottom composition changes from bluff walls to chunk rocks or from chunk rock to pea gravel. "The bigger rocks create a good ambush spot and a lot of times there will be baitfish that run down those banks, and then they hit an edge and it causes them to scatter or get confused."

Transition banks are also easy for Jones to find on a mud-bottom reservoir if it has a well-defined creek channel. Then he looks for steep vertical banks that turn into flats.

A shoreline with mixed rock is usually a transition area where pre-spawn bass take a break along their migration route from their deep-water haunts to the spawning banks.

Cranking Banks for
Pre-spawn Bass

Spring has sprung. The water temperature is rising above the 50-degree mark and pre-spawn bass are moving into the shallows.

"When the water temperature just cracks over the fifty mark, it seems like a ton of fish move shallow," Virginia pro John Crews says. "The bream move up and crappie start moving up, getting ready to spawn. Most of the country also has stained water so the shallow crankbait bite can be absolutely phenomenal that time of year. You can catch some really big fish and some good numbers."

The Bassmaster pro targets the middle to back portions of creeks and keys on transition banks where the contour changes from steep to flat. "A lot of times it correlates with the bottom composition change, where it might go from gravel to red clay or something like that," says Crews. "Those can be key areas where you can catch two or three fish off of (either on the first pass or throughout the course of the day)."

Crews usually casts close to the bank and runs his crankbait less than four feet deep. The Virginia angler notes the proximity of his cast to the shoreline depends on the bank slope. "If it is a real shallow bank I throw a little farther off, but if it is steeper I throw right on the bank."

With his boat positioned parallel to the shoreline, Crews runs his trolling motor at a consistent moderate pace (about forty on the speed dial), which allows him to cover a lot of water. Whenever he finds a change in bank composition or depth, Crews makes multiple presentations to these potential hot spots. He will also run his crankbaits through brush piles in the backs of pockets when the sun is shining. "If there is no sun the fish tend to be on the harder cover such as rocks or bigger logs," he says.

John Crews cranks the shallows to catch pre-spawn bass before the fish move to the spawning banks.

33

Spawning Locations

Whether it's a Northern clear-water natural lake, the tannic waters of Florida, or a Midwestern highland reservoir, largemouth bass can be found spawning in a similar area—a hard-bottom spot sheltered from wind and current.

In the Northern lakes, Jonathon VanDam finds largemouth bedding in canals, small bays, and the back side of main lake points. "Some fish will spawn as deep as twelve feet because the clarity of the lakes is really good," says the Bassmaster pro. He usually finds the males nesting close to small weed clumps or lily pads in the shallows, while the females remain along the first break into deeper water.

Canals and basins protected from the wind are the prime spots BASS pro Shaw Grigsby searches for early spawning fish on Florida waters. The backs of coves and pockets are the first areas bass spawn in impoundments throughout the South and Midwest. "As it gets warmer throughout the spawning season, bass will spawn in just about any cove and down any bank, and the later it gets in the spring then they will be all the way out on the main lake spawning."

While fishing the lakes in his home state of Florida, Grigsby finds bass nesting on any type of hard bottom such as shell beds, gravel, laydown logs, and clumps of lily pad roots. Gravel and chunk rock banks are Grigsby's favorite targets for spawning bass on reservoirs.

Shaw Grigsby looks for a sheltered spot with a hard bottom to find bass during the spawn.

34

Tracking Post-spawn Bass

"When bass come off the beds, there is a time frame when a lot of the fish stay shallow depending on the available cover," says Bassmaster competitor Davy Hite.

Bass remain close to the bank for a couple of weeks after the spawn if a lake has off-colored water or the shallows are filled with cover such as vegetation, stumps, brush piles, standing timber, or boat docks. Hite notices post-spawn bass withdraw quickly to deeper water on clear-water reservoirs with sparse, shallow cover. "Those are places where the fish immediately get on channel drops and ledges," he says. "Once those fish spawn it seems like they just pack up their bags and head out deep."

The South Carolina pro believes post-spawn bass on most bodies of water move to summertime haunts in various stages. The first move is from the spawning bank to a rest stop such as the first available drop-off, which could be a creek channel ledge in five to six feet of water on stained to murky lakes or a river channel drop twenty to twenty-five feet deep on clear impoundments.

The second move depends on food availability. "Bass have gone through the spawning process and recovered and Mother Nature lets them know it is time to feed up and replenish their bodies." So bass might move shallower if bluegill or shad start spawning, or the hungry predators could move out deeper in search of schooling baitfish.

A post-spawn bass' final move is to its summertime haunt, where the fish suspends close to the surface in the early summer because the water's dissolved oxygen level is suitable for both bass and baitfish.

Thick wood cover or weeds will keep bass in the shallows for a couple of weeks after the spawn.

Cranking Shallow for Summer Bass

"A lot of times during the dog days of summer, the deep bite will get kind of finicky, especially in August and September," says Bassmaster Elite Series pro Todd Faircloth. "So then I can go to the very backs of creeks and target laydown logs and stumps and get on a pretty strong pattern."

The Texas pro relies on a square-bill crankbait to catch bass one to four feet deep around shallow wood cover along the flats in the stained water of major creeks. A big log on a flat can be an excellent replenishing spot for summertime bass. "You can just go back and forth on it three or four times throughout the course of the day and catch fish off of it every time," Faircloth says.

The BASS pro casts his crankbait to the far end of a log and employs a high-speed reel (6.1:1 gear ratio) with 17-pound line to burn the lure the entire length of the cover. He tries to bang the crankbait into limbs and keeps cranking after it deflects off the obstacle. "When it hits something and flares off to the left or right is usually when you trigger the bite," says Faircloth.

The tournament veteran believes this tactic is effective because it presents a different look to the fish, which are accustomed to seeing jigs or worms flipped into the wood cover rather than a crankbait banging around in the limbs. He thinks the crankbait also best mimics a large shad or bluegill, the main forage of bass hanging around the shallow wood at that time.

When the dog days of summer arrive, Todd Faircloth targets shallow wood in the backs of creeks with a square-bill crankbait.

36

Summertime Worm Spots

On hot sunny days, Bassmaster Elite Series pro Terry Butcher looks for points with brush piles and ledges to work a magnum-sized plastic worm. The bright sunshine causes the fish to become lethargic and their strike zone shrinks so Butcher wants a lure he can work slowly through the brush and along the ledges.

When bass are suspended or hugging the bottom in brush piles twelve to twenty feet deep, a 10-inch ribbon-tail plastic worm triggers strikes for Butcher. The Oklahoma pro Texas-rigs the worm on 12- to 17-pound fluorocarbon line with a 4/0 offset worm hook and a ⅜- or ½-ounce tungsten steel worm weight.

Most of the brush piles Butcher fishes are on points, although he will also look for some piles between points. Once he finds the brush, Butcher positions his boat on the deep side of the cover and casts his worm beyond it. "I will start the lure out away from it and then try to drag the bait through the pile," Butcher says. "If the brush is really deep I might get over the top of it and jig straight down in it."

Lifting the worm up through the branches and letting it fall back to the bottom allows Butcher to present his lure to fish suspended above the cover or on the lake's floor. "The bite is different every day, so I start out working the worm through there fast, but if I am not getting bites I will slow it down," Butcher says.

The tournament veteran fishes the same Texas-rigged worm along the ledges. He positions his boat in deep water and casts at different angles to the ledge until he finds the sweet spot of the structure. Butcher varies his retrieve until he catches a fish. "A lot of times I will catch them on a really slow drag and sometimes I catch them hopping it," he says.

Terry Butcher works a magnum-sized plastic worm along points with brush and ledges for summertime bass.

37

Sight Fishing for Summer Bass

The summertime heat is still on, but that productive pattern of probing deep brush piles is slowly turning off.

Most summertime bass congregate on offshore structure at depths of twenty-five feet or more, but the deep-water haunts become less reliable by late summer. "As the summer progresses they kind of scatter a little bit," says Alabama pro Steve Kennedy. "I don't know if it is fishing pressure where the guys keep finding them and breaking them up a little bit or if that is just the normal progression.

"Typically the fish are deeper but depending on oxygen levels the fish could be shallow (one foot or less). It is amazing how many fish you can catch in 90- to 100-degree water in one foot of water."

Kennedy's favorite way to catch late summer bass is to go "shallower than most guys would fish." During a Forrest Wood Cup championship on Lake Lanier in August, Kennedy found wolf packs of cruising bass in six to eight inches of clear water in the backs of pockets. "I had to get up where the boat was almost touching the bottom and then throw as far as I could get back there," he recalls. "I was catching 3- to 4-pound class fish."

The Bassmaster Elite Series pro occasionally throws a topwater frog or a buzz bait in the shallows to cover water quickly, but his favorite lure for cruising bass is a watermelon seed 5-inch stick worm impaled on a 4/0- or 5/0 round bend offset hook. For finicky fish, he sometimes downscales to a 4-inch stick worm rigged on a 3/0 hook.

Kennedy occasionally tosses his lure to a stump or other pieces of shallow cover, but most of the time he targets cruising fish. "A lot of times I am sight fishing for them," says Kennedy, who considers bream beds a sweet spot for cruisers.

Steve Kennedy looks for cruising bass or fish holding on stumps and laydowns in extremely shallow water when deep summertime bass fail to cooperate.

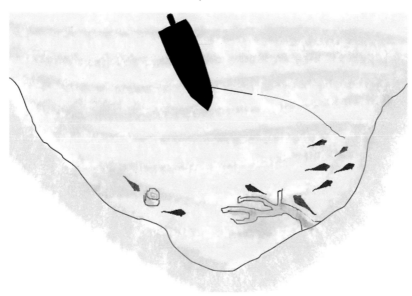

38

Tracking Early Fall Bass

Tracking bass in the early fall reminds BASS pro Stephen Browning of a similar hit-and-miss situation he encounters in the deer woods.

"It's almost like deer hunting, where right before the rut everything gets kind of funky and then all of a sudden everything gets wide open," says Browning. "You go through a short period when the fishing is really tough because you have a lot of shad that are trying to transition and you have a lot of bass that are trying to transition with them, but the major move hasn't come on yet.

"The summertime pattern of deeper brush piles and long points and things like that start playing out (due to the shad movement). Bass are going to be where they can get fat and happy, so the fish will be in the first third of the creek channels and shallower on main lake points."

Browning looks for baitfish in shallower water toward the fronts of the creeks and main lake pockets where the fish have just started migrating from deeper water. "What I normally do is transition to a shallower zone of water," he says. "Whether it is a river system, natural lake, or man-made lake,

I fish from two to eight feet deep instead of that summertime range from eight to eighteen feet out."

Since shad will be feeding heavily on algae in early fall, chunk rocks coated with the green slime are Browning's favorite targets for bass during this time. He searches for chunk rock banks or pea gravel flats that feature a 2- to 3-foot drop-off where bass can quickly move up into the shallows to ambush baitfish.

If the wind is blowing and Browning notices bass are aggressive, he favors burning a lipless crankbait in the shallows. On calm days, Browning opts for a quieter shad-pattern crankbait.

In early fall, bass move to the shallows of main lake points and the front ends of creeks to forage on baitfish.

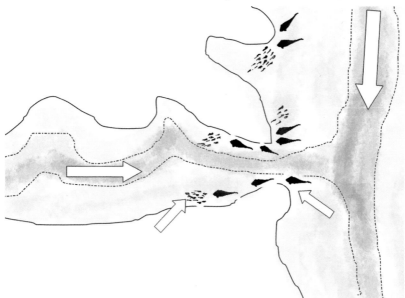

39

Following the Fall Migration

It happens every year, but what actually happens might be contrary to what some anglers have been led to believe.

When the air cools and the nights start getting longer in the fall, bass begin their annual migration to the shallows. The bass migration coincides with shad moving to the shallows, and since so many baitfish show up in the backs of creeks during this time, some anglers perceive that bass throughout the lake have followed the shad into the creeks.

"I don't think the fish necessarily move to the backs of creeks like a lot of people think," says FLW touring pro Greg Bohannon. "I think they just pull up shallower on some of the points and turns just inside the creeks. There are always some resident fish in certain areas, but I think when the shad start migrating to the mouth of the pockets or off the points into the creek arms, the bass definitely take notice and get ready for that fall feeding."

Bassmaster Elite Series pro Todd Faircloth also believes a bass' fall migration route depends on where the fish reside most of the time. "I'm not going to say that all of those fish on the main lake go to the backs of the creeks," says Faircloth. "I think there is a population of fish that live in the major creeks, and when we start having the fall season, 75 percent of the fish that live in that major tributary start going to the backs of the creeks."

Falling water temperature and decreasing hours of daylight seem to trigger the fall migration for baitfish and bass. "If you have a cold snap at that time of the year, it really triggers the fish to start heading that way," Faircloth says. "Even if you don't get a cold snap and have kind of a mild fall, the length of the days plays a factor as well."

The backs of creeks draw baitfish and bass when the leaves turn colors.

40

Fall Migrations on Highland Reservoirs

Greg Bohannon notices highland lake bass start changing locations when the water temperature dips into the high seventies and the action increases as the water drops into the low seventies. "Fishing starts getting considerably better when the fish start pulling out of those summer haunts and get into a little more feeding activity," he says.

Bass suspended over deep trees or drop-offs in the 20- to 30-foot range will move into depths of ten to twelve feet deep and start hugging the bottom in this first stage of the migration. "It seems like they are a lot easier to catch when they start that transition," says Bohannon. He catches these fish on Carolina rigs or football jigs tipped with plastic craws; and as the water continues to cool down and the fish move shallower, the Arkansas pro switches to a Zara Spook or burning a spinnerbait.

During this stage, main lake fish will either move to the primary or secondary points. Bass that gang up on shad in the backs of the creeks are fish that were previously suspended in the timber of the creek channel.

Once the fish reach the shallows, bass remain in the thin water for the remainder of fall. "I think they stay there a good portion of the winter until the water temperature gets down into the forties, and then they get a little more difficult to catch," says Bohannon, who pitches a jig and craw to shallow wood cover and boat docks to catch these fish.

When the water temperature dips into the fifties, some bass start moving back to bluffs and transition banks, so Bohannon throws crankbaits and swim baits until the fish move back into the deep timber and suspend in the treetops for the rest of winter.

Standing timber is a gathering spot for bass migrating to the backs of creeks and coves in the fall.

41

Fall Migrations on Lowland Reservoirs

Bass migration in autumn begins on flatland reservoirs when the water temperature falls into the low seventies. BASS pro Todd Faircloth notices bass in this stage move from the main lake toward the mouth of the creeks, steep drops, secondary points, or creek channel swings. The next phase of the migration occurs when the water temperature drops into the upper sixties and the bass move to the flats three-fourths of the way into the creeks.

During the earliest stage of the migration, Faircloth favors throwing a lipless crankbait that allows him to cover water quickly. When the fish move to the flats, Faircloth continues to throw the lipless crankbait and also tries a square-bill crankbait. The Texas pro first looks for shad on the flats and then looks for potential ambush spots where bass pick off the wandering baitfish. "It is always a better area if there is cover mixed with bait," says Faircloth.

The weather determines how long the fish stay on the flats. "If we have a mild fall, you can catch fish back there for a couple of months," says Faircloth.

As the water continues to cool, the fish start backing out of the creeks along the same route they followed in the beginning of fall. "They have their travel routes," says Faircloth. "They have certain little points or certain little spots that they set up on."

When the fish start moving deeper in the late fall, Faircloth tempts them with a deep-diving crankbait or a football jig tipped with a twin tail plastic grub. The Texas pro notices lowland bass are usually back in their wintertime haunts when the water temperature drops into the fifties.

Todd Faircloth targets flats to catch bass during fall feeding sprees.

42

Autumn Sight Fishing

Sight fishing becomes one of the most effective methods for spawning bass in the spring, but this tactic also produces in the fall when bass migrate to clear, shallow waters.

Texas pro Alton Jones sight fishes in the fall by finding a specific fish holding next to cover and watching for bass following his lure or cruising in the shallows. He notices bass in the fall tend to cruise and feed more than springtime bass, so he works his lures along a stretch of bank and watches for fish following his lures.

Jones believes one of the keys to fall sight fishing is to spot cruising fish at the outer limits of your vision range because the fish are pretty skittish. "Even if they can see you really well, if they are far enough away from you they won't spook yet," says Jones. "So stealth becomes a big part of the game."

Jones's stealth tips include minimizing noise by stepping softly in the boat and making sure his lure enters the water quietly. Operating the trolling motor correctly is another stealth trick Jones employs. If he sees a bass and he's running his trolling motor, Jones keeps his foot on the pedal. "The gut reaction is to take your foot off the trolling motor but that is the instant they will spook," he cautions.

Tempting a sighted fish to bite can be difficult in the fall, so Jones has to be more selective with his lures than he is in the spring. "That time of year is usually a finesse deal for me," he discloses. His favorite lures for fall sight fishing include a 3-inch stick worm on a drop shot rig, a 4-inch stick worm rigged wacky style and a finesse worm (rigged with either a small weight or weightless).

Texas pro Alton Jones sight fishes for bass cruising the shallows in the fall.

43

Stay Shallow for Yuletide Bass

The Yuletide season usually heralds the time when many bass anglers think deep to catch their favorite quarry.

Yet even when it's beginning to look a lot like Christmas, Tracy Adams still keeps in mind a shallow-water option. "It doesn't really matter what time of year it is, there is always going to be a few fish shallow if you can just figure out where they are and what they are doing," says the former Bassmaster Classic qualifier.

The North Carolina pro looks for early winter bass in the shallows about halfway back in the creeks along riprap or natural rock banks. Later in the winter he finds more shallow bass along the main lake rocks adjacent to deep water. The fish in both scenarios will be two to six feet deep along the rocky banks. Adams knows bass will stay in the rocky shallows because the rocks hold heat better and warm the water more than other types of banks.

Some fish can be taken on sunny days when the sunshine warms the rocks, but Adams believes the best days for shallow winter bass are overcast and windy. "If a front is coming in that will be better, but that is just typical of any fishing," says Adams.

Despite the cold, Adams will run and gun a lake until he finds a productive spot. "Then I will beat it to death," he says. "If I catch a couple of good ones off of a place I am going to be there awhile because more fish are there somewhere."

His favorite lures for tempting shallow bass in the winter are a crankbait and a jig. "Most of the time, if I am just on a rock bank, I will throw the crankbait more; if I catch a couple of fish off of a place, I might switch up and throw a jig," says Adams.

Staying shallow on rocky banks is an effective way to catch bass in early winter.

44

Probing Winter Hideouts

A depth change of two feet or twenty feet could be a good wintertime bass hideout to touring pro Dave Wolak.

"The best locations on reservoirs that I have always found are holes," says Wolak. "Fish really group up in holes in the winter if you have a lake where the average depth is less than what is adequate for the fish to stay in a more stable environment."

An example of a wintering hole Wolak targets is a ditch twenty to thirty feet deep in the middle of a long creek arm featuring an expansive flat. The water is too cold on the flat, so the bass seek out the deepest water they can find for a comfort zone. "If you find key vertical cover on parts of that ditch or where there is a lot of forage ganged up, you can really find the bass stacked up," says Wolak.

On a natural shallow lake in Florida, the best winter hideout could be a hole six feet deep at the edge of hydrilla. Wolak notes there might be only a 2-foot drop from the edge of the vegetation into the hole, but the bass seek refuge there because it is the deepest water in the area.

Wolak's favorite wintertime spots vary depending on the body of water. On shallow, lowland reservoirs he looks for cover such as old house foundations, stump rows, and brush piles close to ditches or creek channels.

"In the highland reservoirs I try to get up in the rivers many times to fish the bends and turns that have a lot cleaner rock and a lot more vertical drops (bluff points)," he says.

The North Carolina pro suggests the best winter spots are similar to good summertime haunts. "Points are always good in the winter because that is a magnet for fish that are pulling from somewhere shallow to seek refuge in deeper water."

Dave Wolak finds wintertime bass bunched up on bluff ends.

45

Figuring Out Winter Warm-Ups

Various factors determine how bass react to a winter warm-up on your favorite fishery. Water clarity and forage availability are keys to figuring out how to find bass when winter briefly turns balmy.

Water clarity dictates how much the water temperature will climb on a sunny winter day. Bassmaster Elite Series pro Brian Snowden notices water temperature will rise about two degrees in stained water on a warm and sunny winter day, but the same weather will produce only a one-degree climb in clear water. "If the lake has some stain, I move shallower," he says. "I fish more 45-degree chunk rock banks and go shallow with a ⅜-ounce jig, or I will even catch them on a crankbait."

Snowden's top choice for fishing the chunk rock banks in dirty shallow water is a finesse jig tipped with a plastic chunk trailer. In stained water, Snowden opts for a plastic skirted twin tail grub with a ¼-ounce jighead that he works five to eight feet deep along bluff ends and flats adjacent to a river channel. The chunk rock banks are also ideal spots for Snowden to run a crawfish pattern crankbait.

Pinpointing the depth of baitfish is the key to catching deep bass on clear lakes during a winter warm-up. "Usually when it warms the shad move up and so do the bass," says Snowden. "They move vertically up the water column in the lower clearer section of a reservoir and more horizontally on the upper dirty water sections."

If Snowden notices the shad are moving, he will cast to the baitfish, count his lure down to the same depth or slightly below the baitfish, and then slowly reel his bait back to the boat. His top choice for this deep-water tactic is a 3 ½-inch tube bait with a ¼- or ⅜-ounce ball jighead.

A crawfish pattern crankbait triggers strikes along chunk rock banks during a winter warm-up.

Rock banks are ideal locations to find bass transitioning from the main lake to the coves and vice versa in the spring and fall.

CHAPTER 5

Presentations

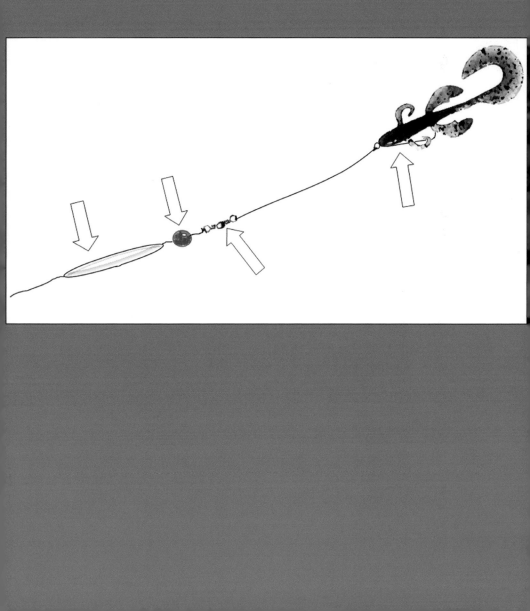

46

Tried-and-True Texas Rig

The touring pros constantly tinker with ways to rig soft plastics, but one standard setup they continue to rely on is the Texas rig.

"One of the key things about a Texas rig is you can fish it through virtually any type of cover," says FLW pro Stacey King. "It is extremely weedless and you can fish it with any kind of soft plastic."

The Missouri angler notes the Texas rig has been a complement of the plastic worm for more than fifty years, since the setup can be fished from the shallows out to extremely deep water. Some pros have been rigging their plastic worms or other soft plastics on jigheads for fishing in open water, but King still favors the Texas rig when he needs to deliver his soft plastics into heavy cover.

A Texas rig mostly produces for King in the warmer months, although he has caught bass on Texas-rigged beaver-style baits when the water is cold. King's rig includes bullet weights ranging from ¼- or 5/16-ounce for fishing small soft plastics and shallow to ½-ounce for working large plastic worms along ledges during the post-spawn. King favors a 5/0 round-bend offset hook for Texas-rigging 10-inch worms and scales down to a number one or two hook for finesse worms.

The versatility of the Texas rig allows King to retrieve his soft plastics in a variety of ways. "You just have to experiment and see how the fish want it, whether they want a fast or slow retrieve or hopping it," he says. " I have caught them on Texas rigs using an extremely slow drag retrieve, and on the other end of the spectrum, I have caught fish jerking it hard, ripping it up off the bottom, and letting it fall back to create a strike."

A Texas-rigged soft plastic is still one of the best options for catching quality bass in heavy cover.

47

Tiny Weights for Texas Rigs

When his finesse worm presentations need a change of pace or direction, tournament veteran Marty Stone adds a little weight to the subject.

When using a floating worm, Stone slips on a diminutive sinker to the front of his Texas rig in certain situations to make the worm slowly fall and trigger more strikes. The North Carolina pro mostly uses his mini-weights in the spring when the fish are spawning or lingering in the shallows during the post-spawn.

Stone's mini-weight Texas rig consists of a 1/64- or 1/32-ounce worm weight and a floating worm impaled on a 2/0 thin wire offset hook. "Some people ask why even bother using a weight," he says. "You would be surprised though how that little 1/64- or 1/32-ounce weight will sink the lure a little bit faster than just a hook and a worm."

That little extra weight also makes the worm's tail throb more as it pulls the nose of the lure downward. Stone has discovered this slow-falling worm with the tantalizing tail is especially appealing to hefty female bass recuperating from the spawn. "You want that fish to be able to ease over without expending much effort and have a real easy meal," he said.

"They really haven't gotten into that post-spawn feed mode either. They are still back in the places where they spawned, but they are off the bed and have quit biting."

Since he wants his worm to skip under docks and around wood cover, Stone keeps his weight snug against the worm. He skips his worms on a 6-foot, 10-inch spinning rod with 6- or 8-pound fluorocarbon line.

Stone skips the lure into the shady spots of the dock and lets it fall to the bottom, hops it once, and lets it fall before retrieving the worm. Most of his strikes occur on the initial fall.

Texas-rigging a floating worm with a tiny weight tricks post-spawn bass into biting.

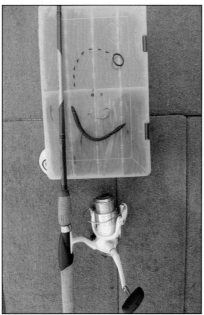

48

Carolina Rigging after the Spawn

Trying to pinpoint post-spawn bass can still be a guessing game despite all the sophisticated electronics we have available today.

Touring pro Peter Thliveros takes a lot of the guesswork out of finding fish migrating back to their deep-water haunts by dragging a Carolina rig. "It is a tool that covers a lot of water efficiently, but you can fish it slow and still cover a lot of water," says Thliveros.

The Florida angler favors rigging on flats with scattered stumps, grass, or small rock piles. A 6-inch plastic lizard and 10-inch plastic worm in green pumpkin, watermelon, and watermelon-red flake hues are Thliveros' favorite lures for rigging. "I like lures that present a pretty good profile," said Thliveros, who sometimes throws an 8-inch lizard when he needs to catch a kicker fish.

The components of Thliveros' rig include a ⅝-ounce Mojo-style tungsten sinker, followed by a bead and a swivel on a main line of 17-pound fluorocarbon. Just about any size swivel will work on the rig, according to the Florida pro.

"When you have a big old hunk of tungsten and a bead in front of it, the size of the swivel isn't going to matter," said Thliveros.

Post-spawn bass tend to be lethargic after the rigors of spawning, so Thliveros prefers using a longer leader (three feet) in warmer water. The fish will usually be roaming from the cover or suspended off the bottom during the post-spawn, so when the sinker on a rig with a longer leader hits the cover, the lure glides away from the target to trigger strikes from the roaming fish.

Thliveros opts for a heavy leader line (15-pound test fluorocarbon) so he can drag his rig through the cover, especially when the sinker makes contact with either stumps or rocks. Tied on the end of his leader is a 4/0 hook.

When he needs to cover a lot of water to find post-spawn bass, Peter Thliveros relies on a Carolina-rigged plastic lizard.

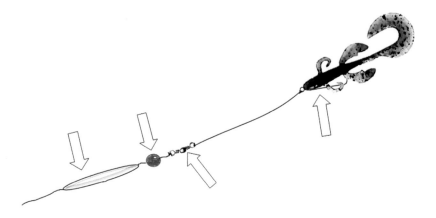

49

Split Shotting for Shallow Bass

A Carolina rig is ideal for bumping a soft plastic along the bottom in deep water, but when bass move to the shallows during the pre-spawn and spawn, a mini-version of the rig works better.

Missouri pro Stacey King has been a longtime advocate of the split-shot or Mojo rig for catching shallow springtime bass along gravel pockets and chunk rock banks. "It is just a real effective technique for black bass when they are in shallow water [one to ten feet deep]," he says. "It is basically a light Carolina rig." He notes the rig is most effective in clear water and heavy fishing pressure situations.

King originally used split shots for his weights but now relies on the Mojo-style cylindrical weight, which tends to hang up less than the split shot. A ¼-ounce weight is the sinker King depends on most often because it consistently stays in contact with the bottom. He occasionally scales down to a ⅛-ounce for finicky fish and sometimes uses a heavier weight when fishing in the wind.

Similar to the Carolina rig, the Mojo setup features the weight positioned various distances from the hook and lure. King usually keeps his hook about sixteen to eighteen inches behind the weight so that the sinker stays in contact with the bottom but the lure can still float free. The slip sinker is held in place by a couple of rubber band strands that King inserts into the weight with a threading tool.

A 6-inch plastic lizard is King's favorite lure for dragging behind a Mojo weight. He also hooks 4- and 5-inch finesse worms or small plastic crawfish on his Mojo rigs. The tournament veteran either drags the rig slowly across the bottom or employs a pumping motion with his rod to make the lure slightly lift and fall.

Dragging a split-shot or Mojo rig along the bottom of clear, shallow water coaxes skittish bass into biting.

50

Rattling Drop Shot Rig

Bass are being force-fed a steady diet of finesse baits throughout the country, as nearly every savvy bass angler keeps some light spinning tackle in his boat's rod box and carries an assortment of finesse baits on board. So the pros must continue to find new finesse tactics or refine the old reliable techniques to survive on today's highly competitive tournament trails.

Alabama pro Gerald Swindle enhances his drop-shot rig by using a rattling weight consisting of a tungsten ball that he has encased in 3/16- or 1/4-ounce lead cylindrical weights. He ties a number one straight shank hook about ten to twelve inches above the weight on 6- or 8-pound fluorocarbon line and impales either a finesse worm or small plastic craw on the hook.

Since he is targeting suspended fish along bluffs, standing timber or bridge columns, Swindle employs a vertical jigging presentation with the noisy weight to attract the fish to his rig. "As you are moving it, the weight has a really nice sound to it," he says. "I drop the rig down into the zone I want, kick the reel into gear, and hold the line tight and shake it. That way I am getting some sound out of that weight and some action out of that worm."

The rattling weight rig also triggers strikes from bottom-hugging fish along ledges. Swindle pitches the drop shot to a ledge and lets it fall to the bottom, then shakes it to stir up the bottom and create the fish-attracting rattle. "I want that sound every time I move it," he says.

The key to this presentation is to barely shake the rod to impart action to the bait and generate sound from the rattle. However, he cautions, "If you catch yourself shaking that rod more than six to ten inches, you are way overfishing it."

Alabama pro Gerald Swindle depends on a drop-shot rig with a rattling weight to trigger strikes from bottom-hugging bass.

Super-Sizing Baits for Drop Shots

Today's fishing pressure has turned many bass into finicky eaters, so anglers have resorted to downsizing their lures and tackle to coax bites. The drop shot rig has emerged from this trend as one of the most effective ways to present a thin, 3- or 4-inch lure to a passive bass.

However there are still plenty of times when bass prefer their meals super-sized, and tournament trail pros have discovered the drop shot rig can also effectively deliver a big, bulky dinner to a heavyweight bass. "It's the same principle behind drop shotting no matter what size bait you are throwing," says Dion Hibdon, the former Bassmaster Classic and FLW Tour champion from Missouri. "It's giving your bait a totally different look to the fish. It's a really natural-looking presentation."

When fishing gets tough and Hibdon needs a kicker fish, the cast-for-cash angler supersizes his drop shot rig with a 5- to 6-inch flipping tube, a 9-inch ring worm, or a 10-inch paddle tail worm. He selects a 4/0 or 5/0 wide gap hook for his flipping tube and a 4/0 or 5/0 hook for his 9- and 10-inch plastic worms. Most of the time, Hibdon uses ⅜- or ½-ounce weights for his magnum drop shot rig, although he opts for ¾- and 1-ounce versions when punching the lures through weed mats or working the rig in deep water.

Drop shotting big baits produces best for Hibdon in the summer and fall in waters with visibility of at least one to two feet. The Missouri pro's drop shot with the worm produces bass from brush piles whenever the fish start ignoring his Texas-rigged worm. "If you have caught fish day after day out of those brush tops and the fish stop biting, then slip a drop shot in there," advises Hibdon.

A magnum-sized plastic worm rigged on a drop shot produces for Dion Hibdon when pressured bass are in brush piles.

Jumbo Drop Shot for Offshore Structure

A jumbo drop-shot rig produces for Bassmaster Mega-bucks winner Alton Jones when he wants an alternative to a Carolina rig on big-bass lakes. "One of the keys is that you can bring that bait up off the bottom with a drop shot, and when you feed it slack, it falls just like a weightless bait for a more natural presentation," says Jones. "It is a slow, enticing, undulating movement and you get more movement with a big bait than you do a small bait."

His supersize choices for drop shotting include a 4-inch tube bait, 10-inch worm, and a soft plastic craw. He selects a 1-ounce bullet or egg-shaped weight and holds it in place with a barrel swivel tied below the sinker. The Texas pro uses a longer drop (three to four feet) than the gap on most conventional drop shots.

The oversized drop-shot rig gives Jones an added summertime weapon when bass stop biting Carolina- or Texas-rigged soft plastics and deep-diving crankbaits. "If I have a sweet spot that is holding fish and they quit biting, I fire this rig in there and pick off several extra fish and, a lot of times, big fish," says Jones.

The tournament veteran retrieves his drop-shot setup along any offshore structure where he normally drags a Carolina rig. When he thinks his lure is in a sweet spot, Jones tries to pull up his bait without lifting the weight off the bottom. Then he lets his line go slack, which allows the lure to fall back to the bottom and keeps the weight in the same location. This tactic lets Jones impart a lot of action to his lure without moving it out of the sweet spot.

"I fish it probably a little slower than a Carolina rig and don't necessarily make as long of a cast with it," describes Jones.

Alton Jones tricks offshore bass with a magnum drop-shot rig when the fish stop biting Texas- and Carolina-rigged soft plastics and deep-diving crankbaits.

Alabama Rig Options

The umbrella rig has been used for a long time for trolling for striped bass, but a variation of that setup became the rage of bass fishing when Paul Elias won a $100,000 FLW Tour Open on Lake Guntersville.

Although banned in some states and by some bass clubs, the Alabama rig, equipped with its five wires for a multiple lure presentation, is still a hot item among both tournament competitors and recreational anglers.

Swimbaits are most frequently matched with the Alabama rig, but other lures will also work on the device. "The sky is the limit for whatever you want to throw," says FLW pro Dan Morehead. The Kentucky pro varies the size of the jigheads for his lures from ⅛-ounce to ½-ounce depending on the application and depth he is fishing.

His lure colors depend on water clarity or weather conditions. "If I am fishing a clear body of water and the wind is not blowing very much or there is sunshine, then I go to more translucent colors; but if it is cloudy or windy, I will go to brighter colors like white," he says.

Morehead's favorite time to sling a rig is during the pre-spawn when bass are shallow. "I like a sunshiny day with pretty good wind that puts a pretty good chop on the water," he says. "I think they can see it better on a sunny day and they will come from a farther distance to get it."

The retrieve Morehead employs for the Alabama rig varies on the conditions and depth of the fish. "The whole key is to find out what depth the fish are suspended and maintaining that cadence with the retrieve," says Morehead. "Usually it is just a slow, steady retrieve. It seems like the more action you try to impart on the bait, the less bites you get."

Swimbaits are the lures the pros usually choose for their Alabama rigs.

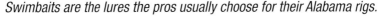

54

Shaky Head Choices

The growing popularity of shaky head fishing has prompted tackle manufacturers to create a wide array of jighead sizes and styles. "One of the keys to shaky head fishing is that you want to use as light of a head as possible and still keep in contact with the bottom," says Jimmy Mason, a Bassmaster Open competitor and Alabama guide. He opts for three types of head designs for shaking his soft plastics.

When fishing in rocks and open water, Mason favors a ball head jig. "That round jig gives the bait a rocking action as you are working it through the cover, since that head rolls back and forth," he says.

Mason usually selects these jigheads in ⅛- or ³⁄₁₆-ounce sizes for most applications, but he will switch to a ¼-ounce version when fishing in the wind, current, or water deeper than twenty feet. His favorite lures to attach to this style of shaky head are 4- and 6-inch finesse worms or a 4-inch stick worm. He likes to throw the stick worm on a shaky head whenever shad are present because the combo creates a darting action similar to that of the baitfish.

A standup jighead is Mason's choice for shaking finesse worms and soft plastic twitch baits along riprap and other broken rock bottoms. He favors this style of head because it slides through the rocks with minimal hang-ups, and he can fish the worm slowly without much shaking since the jighead keeps the worm standing up straight. The $\frac{1}{8}$- and $\frac{3}{16}$-ounce jigheads work best for most of Mason's shaky head tactics in the rocks, although he will switch to a $\frac{5}{16}$-ounce head for probing deep water.

When he wants to deliver a shaky worm into heavy cover, Mason selects a snag-resistant standup jighead with a keeper attachment in a $\frac{1}{8}$-ounce size. The Alabama guide resorts to a $\frac{3}{32}$-ounce model for skimming his worm over the top of shallow grass.

A standup jighead is ideal for shaky head presentations along riprap and other broken rock bottoms.

The type of bank and cover he is fishing determines which style of shaky jighead Jimmy Mason uses for his finesse fishing tactics.

CHAPTER 6

Soft Plastics

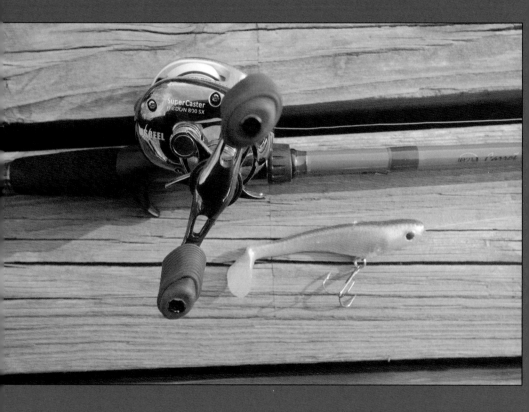

55

Swimming a Worm

When bass are suspended in standing timber or submerged vegetation during the pre-spawn and post-spawn, veteran tournament angler Marty Stone favors swimming a 7 ½-inch sickle tail plastic worm for these fish.

"You run into certain situations in the pre-spawn and the post-spawn where the fish don't want a lot of erratic movement," says Stone. "When I throw that worm out there I count it down to whatever depth of the cover I am fishing (usually five feet deep over a depth of ten feet). Then I use a nice steady retrieve."

The North Carolina pro believes rigging is the whole key to swimming a worm. He favors 15-pound fluorocarbon line because fluorocarbon sinks and allows him to swim the worm deeper. The worm weight is also critical in controlling the depth of the worm. A light weight makes the worm fall too slowly to the proper depth and the worm also starts rising too much when it's retrieved. If there is a slight wind, Stone matches his worm with a ¼-ounce tungsten weight, but in stronger winds or if he wants the worm to run deeper he selects a $5/16$-ounce sinker. He attaches the worm to a 5/0 offset round bend hook.

Using the right rod is another key to the presentation. Stone depends on a 7 ½-foot light action rod that allows him to make long-distance casts with the worm. A medium-speed baitcast reel is best for swimming a worm since Stone wants to make sure he retrieves the worm at a slow clip. "If you are going to err at all on this retrieve, err on the slow side," says Stone. "If you err on the fast side you are going to bring it way above the fish too soon."

Tournament pro Marty Stone swims a worm over submerged weeds for pre-spawn and post-spawn bass.

56

Buzzing a Worm

Buzzing a soft plastic frog across the surface is a deadly topwater tactic in many situations, but there are times when a worm with a lively tail can be more effective. Former FLW touring pro Brennan Bosley uses 8-inch paddle tail and sickle tail worms (in June bug or other dark colors) whenever he wants to buzz a soft plastic through thick surface cover, such as a patch of reeds, because the worms have a smaller profile and snake through the cover easier than a frog bait. He also recommends buzzing a worm as a follow-up tactic when bass continue to short strike a plastic frog.

The pace is fast and the strikes can be furious when buzzing a worm through vegetation. "I tend to keep it buzzing," says Bosley. "A lot of times it is a good technique during the post-spawn when the fish are guarding fry. You can buzz right over the top of where they are bedding in the reeds or wads of grass."

The Arkansas angler rigs the buzzing worm with a ⅟₃₂-ounce Florida-style screw-in sinker to keep the worm close to the weight so it will slide through lily pads and reeds easier. He favors matching the worm with a 5/0 hook because the larger hook increases the chances for a better hookset during the high-speed retrieve.

Braided line works best for Bosley when he buzzes a worm through weeds. He sometimes uses 50-pound test, but favors 30-pound test most of the time because it is easier to cast. His worm buzzing tackle includes a 7.1:1 gear ratio baitcast reel to handle the fast retrieve and a flipping stick for hauling fish out of the thick cover.

Buzzing a paddle tail worm through vegetation can be a deadly topwater tactic.

(Photo courtesy of Zoom Bait Company)

57

Dead Sticking a Lizard

Dragging a plastic lizard along the bottom on a Texas or Carolina rig can be a very effective method for catching bass through the warm months, but when the water is cold, bass sometimes prefer a dead, still presentation of this soft plastic.

As the water temperature rises into the 50- to 55-degree range during early spring, Bassmaster pro Pete Ponds catches a bass' curiosity by dead sticking (letting a lure sit still for an extended time) a Carolina-rigged 6-inch plastic lizard.

Ponds' dead sticking tactic works best in clear water along points where the Mississippi pro throws his rig into a depth of five to six feet. His rig consists of a ¾-ounce weight followed by a 2 ½-foot leader with a green pumpkin or watermelon plastic lizard.

The Elite Series pro believes that the splash of the weight while hitting the water and the disturbance it makes while landing on the bottom arouses a bass' curiosity. "When the weight hits they hear that, and then they swim over to see it," he says. "It is almost like the weight draws the attention of the fish when I don't ever move it. If I move it, I don't get a strike."

Letting the lizard sit for up to one minute might seem like an eternity to others, but Ponds knows dead sticking that long can be productive. "When dead sticking a bait, you have to have total confidence in what you are doing," he says. "I have found that the longer you can stand to do it, the better off you are. When you first start doing it, you might think you are just wasting your time. Once you get a strike and the more confidence you build, it feels like you are really fishing when you are doing that."

Letting a Carolina-rigged plastic lizard sit still on the bottom for up to a minute produces strikes from curious pre-spawn bass.

Plastic Lizards for Spawning Bass

A spawning bass will gently pick up any soft plastic lure and move the bait out of its nest, but the fish will smash a plastic lizard when it enters a nest. "It is a good bait when bass get on beds because bass don't like a lizard for some reason," says BASS pro Tommy Biffle. "They might think it is a waterdog or something like that robbing their eggs."

Plastic lizards usually range in size from four to eight inches, but Biffle favors the 8-inch version for bedding bass. "The old saying goes that bigger baits catch bigger fish," says Biffle. "If that 8-inch lizard gets around a big bass, that fish is going to get it." Biffle's favorite plastic lizard colors are plum and black neon for fishing dirty water or green pumpkin and watermelon-red flake for clear-water situations.

When sight fishing for bedding bass, Biffle prefers his plastic lizard on a Texas rig with a ⁵⁄₁₆-ounce worm weight most of the time, although he will scale down to a ¼-ounce weight for extremely shallow nests. Since the plastic lizard Biffle uses has a hollow body, he inserts a foam ear plug into the bait to make it float off the bottom and stand up in the nest to imitate an intruder eating eggs. "You can drag it up there in the bed and just sit there and shake, shake, shake it and it will just keep moving," says Biffle, who impales his magnum lizard on a 5/0 extra wide gap offset worm hook. "Those fish can't stand that."

Tommy Biffle inserts foam into his plastic lizards to make the baits stand up in a bass' nest.

59

Captivating Creatures

When water temperatures climb above the 60-degree mark, BASS pro Greg Hackney tempts bass with soft plastic creatures or Hawg-style baits "They are the best of both worlds," says Hackney. "They have the bulk of a jig but they also have all that action and appeal of a [plastic] worm." The Louisiana angler favors this style of soft plastic because its appendages and flappers generate a lot of swimming action and its bulkiness is appealing to bigger bass.

Flipping a Texas-rigged creature bait into heavy cover is Hackney's favorite way to fish this soft plastic. When targeting bass on beds, Hackney matches his lure with a pegged ¼- or ⅜-ounce tungsten bullet weight, but as the water gets warmer and the fish move into brush piles or deep timber, he switches to a weight as heavy as a one-half ounce to make the bait sink faster and trigger reaction strikes.

Hackney impales a 4-inch creature on a 4/0 hook tied to 15-pound fluorocarbon line when he fishes clear water. He opts for a 5/0 or 6/0 hook for flipping 5-inch creatures on 50-pound braid in off-color water. His flipping tackle consists of a 7 ½-foot medium-heavy rod and a 7.1:1 baitcast reel.

Dead sticking a creature bait produces best for Hackney during the spawn. "I like to pitch it to the targets and not move it for a while," he says. "That has a tendency to irritate those fish." In the summertime, bass need less coaxing, so Hackney allows the lure fall into the cover, hops it once or twice, and then reels it in to pitch to another target.

Touring pro Greg Hackney selects a creature or hawg-style bait when flipping for big bass in heavy cover.

60

Craw Worms Imitating Shad

A Texas-rigged craw worm has been a staple of flipping specialist Tommy Biffle for years on the tournament trail, but the Oklahoma pro also relies on it as a jig trailer when bass feed heavily on shad in the fall.

During autumn, Biffle wants his lure to emulate a baitfish so he selects a ⅜-ounce white jig tipped with a smoke-silver craw worm. He pinches about a quarter of an inch off the craw's tail and threads the hook so the point comes out in the middle of the fat part of the craw.

Keying on flooded bushes and boat docks, Biffle pitches to his targets and employs a pumping retrieve to make the lure swim around the cover. "If you are throwing at buck bushes, the strike could come anywhere; if you are throwing around docks, the bite usually comes around a break in the Styrofoam or on the corners," he says.

The BASS veteran swims his lure near the bottom of the dock's foam and occasionally lets it drop below the foam to trigger a reaction strike. Bass tend to short strike his jig-and-craw combo when he's fishing docks, so Biffle sometimes adds a trailer hook. He uses a treble hook that he cuts off one bend and positions it on the jig hook so that the remaining hook points ride upward while swimming the lure.

When he wants to flip the bushes with a smaller profile lure, Biffle opts for a smoke-silver Texas-rigged craw worm (4/0 hook and pegged $\frac{5}{16}$-ounce tungsten weight). The mood of the fish determines whether Biffle swims the Texas-rigged craw or lets it stay in the cover. "If they are biting well, they will get it on the first drop, but sometimes I'll have to pump it up and down several times," he says.

Tommy Biffle opts for a silver-flaked craw worm when he needs to use a shad imitator in the fall.

61

Soft Jerk Baits for Cruisers

When bass are cruising the shallows in the spring and fall, Jonathon VanDam tempts these fish with a soft plastic jerk bait. "It really imitates a baitfish about as well as any lure," says the Michigan pro. "It is a very effective lure when the bass are up shallow chasing baitfish. It has a real erratic action so it never does the same thing and that really fires up bass."

The Bassmaster Elite Series competitor dotes on a 5-inch soft jerk bait for his shallow-water presentations. He rigs the lure Texas style on a 4/0 straight-shank worm hook with a slight variation from the way most anglers set up the bait. "I actually rig it upside down (flat side down) because it really gives it more of a side-to-side action," he says. "You can also reel it fast and it swims like a swimbait."

VanDam's favorite colors for soft jerk baits depend on the available forage. If he is fishing waters where the primary forage is sunfish, VanDam prefers blue and green hues for his jerk bait, but if shad are the bass' main food source, he opts for white or blue-and-pearl colors.

A quick, erratic retrieve produces best for VanDam. "I like to twitch the rod on slack line and get that thing to dart back and forth," says VanDam, who works the lure on 12-pound fluorocarbon with a 6-foot, 10-inch medium-heavy casting rod and a 7.1:1 baitcast reel. "I like to give it a few twitches and then pause it and then give it a few more twitches. I try to mix it up and never do the same cadence twice."

Rigging the lure upside down produces more side-to-side action on Jonathon VanDam's soft plastic jerk bait.

62

Dead Sticking Soft Jerk Baits

Wintertime schooling bass fall for a dead sticking presentation that Texas pro Kelly Jordon employs with a soft plastic jerk bait. He favors this lure for dead sticking because its flat tail wiggles as it falls with a 5/0 weighted wide gap hook. Using line as heavy as 17-pound test allows Jordon's lure to fall slower and ensures a better hookup when he has to stick a fish with the magnum-sized hook.

Jordon targets winter bass suspended near tree rows fifteen to twenty feet deep over depths of thirty-five to forty feet. The Texas angler has also caught suspended bass on his dead sticking tactics along bridge pilings, bluffs, and dam walls. "Those suspended fish are some of the hardest fish to catch but that is a deadly presentation for them," he says.

After he finds the suspended fish with his electronics, Jordon casts out his jerk bait to the edge of the tree rows. "I just let it sink until they hit it, and one hits it about every time," says Jordon. "I have let it sink for fifteen seconds or more." He believes dead sticking the lure gives it the appearance of a wounded shad as it slowly descends into the schooling bass. Jordon thinks the slow-falling jerk bait is more effective in this situation than a suspending stick bait because the soft plastic lure can probe deeper and fall straight down into the schools, whereas the stick bait fails to reach the strike zone even when the lure attains its maximum diving depth.

If he needs to dead stick for fish deeper than twenty feet, Jordon attaches his jerk bait to a ¼- or ⅜-ounce jighead. He lets the jig and soft jerk bait fall on a slack line without imparting any rod movement. "The bow in the line will really slow the lure down once it gets twenty feet or so," says Jordon.

When Kelly Jordon finds wintertime bass suspended in trees, he dead sticks a soft plastic jerk bait to catch the lethargic fish.

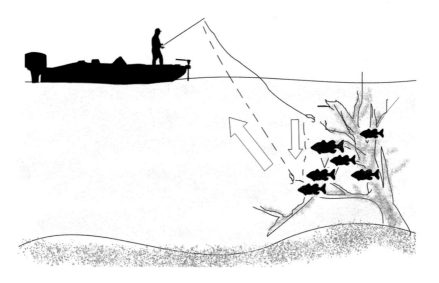

63

Two-Way Tube

Bassmaster pro Shaw Grigsby believes a tube bait is one of the most versatile lures an angler can own. "Everything will eat it because it represents both a shad and a crawfish," says Grigsby. "What is unique about it is that it has that long cylindrical shape like a shad." The Florida angler notes the tube can also be crawled and hopped along the bottom to mimic a crawfish. Grigsby's favorite tube colors are green pumpkin for clear water; black neon and black/blue for stained water; and white for sight fishing in the spring and to imitate shad in the fall.

The tube works for Grigsby either as a finesse lure for fishing in clear water with spinning tackle (6-foot, 10-inch medium-heavy rod and spinning reel filled with 6- to 10-pound line) or as a power bait for flipping into heavy cover with a 7 ½-foot flipping stick and 20- to 25-pound fluorocarbon line. Grigsby sets up his tubes on a Texas rig with a ³⁄₁₆- or ¼-ounce bullet weight and either a 5/0 or 6/0 flipping-style hook for heavy cover situations or a 4/0 wide gap tube hook for his finesse tactics.

When sight fishing, Grigsby tosses his tube past a bass' nest and slowly crawls the lure along the bottom up to the bed to imitate a small crawfish invader. For his flipping presentation, Grigsby lets the tube sink to the bottom, then shakes and pops it a couple of times before lifting it out of the cover to try another target.

A tube bait serves as both a crawfish and shad imitator for tournament veteran Shaw Grigsby.

64

Grubbing for Bass

A plastic grub has been a longtime favorite of panfish anglers and has a following among some of the top bass pros. "It is a lure that worked thirty years ago and will work thirty years from now," says plastic grub advocate Tim Horton.

The Alabama pro favors a 5-inch curly-tail plastic grub especially when he is fishing clear-water highland reservoirs. "It is a natural minnow-type swimming presentation," he says. "When you put it on a jighead, it has a good natural look coming through the water. It is a great lure to throw for schooling fish when largemouth are busting shad on the surface."

Horton's favorite situation for throwing a plastic grub is when largemouth bass are suspended over deep water on sunny, calm days in the late winter, early spring, and summer. He finds these fish along points and boat docks and in standing timber where the trees are sitting in sixty feet of water and top out at twenty feet.

A ball-head jig matches up well with a plastic grub, but Horton prefers sticking his grub on a darter head jig. "I like how [the grub] swims a little better because it is streamlined with that cone head [of the darter jig]," says Horton. He opts for a ¼-ounce jighead most of the time, although he occasionally relies on a ½-ounce version for swimming his grub in the deep trees. His favorite grub colors include natural hues such as green pumpkin, watermelon, and smoke with blue flake.

Horton casts out his grub and counts it down to the depth he saw the suspended fish on his graph. Then he employs a slow, steady retrieve with an occasional pause and a twitch of the rod tip. Since suspended fish are usually lethargic, Horton makes sure not to impart too much action with his grub.

Swimming a plastic grub through schools of bass suspended over deep water produces for Tim Horton on calm, sunny days.

65

Stick Worm Basics

The stick worm looks rather plain while hanging on a hook, but when submerged in water, this lure's seductive wiggling tail will tempt even the most finicky bass into biting.

The Senko (the original stick worm created by Gary Yamamoto) has to be considered one of the simplest and most effective lures for catching bass today, yet some anglers have a tendency to overdo it with the lure. They diminish the effectiveness of the Senko by matching the lure with tackle that is too heavy or working the lure too fast.

While some anglers have success wacky rigging the Senko, Yamamoto prefers his Senko on a weightless Texas rig with a 3/0 extra wide gap hook. "I think some people use too big of a hook because they are thinking the bigger hook they use the better chance they have of hooking the fish," says Yamamoto. "That does work at times, but then sometimes with a bigger hook, they lose the action of the bait on the fall and half the time they lose the bait because it tears off."

The lure designer believes smaller, light wire hooks increase the lure's tail action and make the Senko last longer, as the bait slides easier up the hook and onto the line while fighting a fish. Yamamoto also recommends rigging the Senko on a circle hook that embeds in a fish's mouth by merely reeling after the bite.

The Senko is ideal for casting to any targets since its slow fall keeps it in the strike zone longer and it is weedless when rigged Texas style. Yamamoto employs a simple lift-and-drop retrieve to tempt bass. "It's like working a plastic worm but not quite as fast because it takes longer for it to fall," he describes.

Despite its plain looks, a stick worm has a seductive tail action that appeals to bass.

66

Stick Worms for Spawning Bass

Soft plastics are hard to beat when you need to trick bass on the beds.

The problem is several soft plastics will work so how do you decide which to use most often? The touring pros usually let water conditions dictate which lures and colors to try. When sight fishing in clear water, many pros rely on a stick worm in a bright color they can see or a natural hue.

Bassmaster Elite Series star Brent Chapman throws a Texas-rigged stick worm in green or green/red flake hues on a 4/0 worm hook. "I try to use it without weight but sometimes I put a ¹⁄₁₆- or ⅛-ounce weight on it if it is windy or if I am fishing it in a little deeper water," says Chapman.

If he sees a fish on a bed, the Kansas pro will mark the location of the bass and back off to where the fish is out of sight. Then he makes a blind cast to the spot he marked and lets the lure fall without imparting any action to it. "The less you do with it the better," he says. "Typically I throw it out and count it down to whatever depth and then I kind of raise up on it. I may let it fall a second but then I just like to reel it in and make another cast."

When sight fishing open water flats, Oklahoma pro Fred Roumbanis relies on a stick worm in a tilapia hue and rigs it wacky style. If he is targeting grass, Roumbanis Texas-rigs his stick worm with a ⅛-ounce tungsten weight.

After pitching to a hole in the grass, Roumbanis lets the stick worm fall to the bottom. "Then I kind of shake it a little bit, pull slowly, and shake it again," he says.

When sight fishing on open flats, Fred Roumbanis rigs a stick worm wacky style to catch bedding bass.

67

Backward Stick-Worm Rig

Attaching a stick worm to a jighead usually has some hang-ups in thick cover, so Tim Horton solves this problem by designing a special rig with a stick worm impaled Texas style on a 4/0 hook without any weight placed on the front of the lure. Instead Horton sticks a special weight he makes into the worm's tail. "The weights are just poured, collared jigheads without putting the hooks in them, so it makes them a ball weight with a collar," he describes.

The collared weight can also be made by snipping the hooks off of ball jigheads. The collar is the key since it allows Horton to keep the weight snug to the worm's tail even when casting the lure.

The Alabama pro selects ¼- to ½-ounce weights depending on the thickness of the cover. "You can flip bushes with a ¼-ounce weight with this system where you can't get a ¼-ounce weight in the heavy cover if it were Texas-rigged or pegged the other way because of how the lure has to turn and pull the line down," he says.

The weighted tail causes the worm to fall straight down and pull the line into the cover, whereas a worm with weight on its head tends to pendulum away from the target. This rig allows Horton to make a softer presentation to the cover since he can use a lighter weight and the lure will fall straight down into the bass' lair.

The backward rig also prevents line abrasion during the hook set. "When you set the hook and the weight is up with the line tie, the line pulls up against the brush and it roughens the line, but with this rig the lure doesn't have to turn, it just comes straight out," says Horton.

A backward Texas rig allows Tim Horton to drop stick worms straight down into thick cover without hanging up.

68

Plastic Frog Explosions

"Grass and bass go together and a [plastic] frog is right there with them," says BASS pro Stephen Browning. "It is a very versatile, weedless, topwater bait. A frog seems to be one of those baits that you can put just about anywhere and catch fish on it in any situation (grass, docks, laydowns, standing timber). You have to be crazy not to like the explosion created by a frog."

Browning employs a walk-the-dog style retrieve when working his frog in openings of a weed mat or along tules. He makes a slight modification to the frog to improve its walking action. "I cut one leg a quarter of an inch shorter than the other so the longer leg will have a little different water resistance on one side to help the nose of that bait tilt a little bit and make the frog go side to side better." When fishing heavy cover, Browning also likes to insert a rattle into the hollow body of the frog so the added noise will make it easier for bass to hone in on the lure.

Since he usually places his frog into thick vegetation, Browning relies on stout tackle (7-foot, 1-inch medium-heavy rod and baitcast reel filled with 50-pound braid) to winch a bass out of its weedy lair.

This bass exploded on a plastic frog walked along the surface.

69

Buzzing Toads

Whenever he fishes matted or submerged vegetation in the fall, Kansas pro Brent Chapman prefers a silver-flake soft plastic toad rather than a buzz bait for running over the weeds. "It is way more consistent," says Chapman. "It doesn't ball up in the vegetation like a buzz bait does."

The BASS veteran slips a glass bead on his line and ties on a 5/0 hook to stick into his frog. He secures the glass bead in front of the frog's nose with a bobber stop to prevent slime from balling up on the hook eye and knot.

With the frog running at a steady pace to keep its legs flapping on the surface, Chapman targets both the surface mat and the weed edges in water less than five feet deep. "That is just something you have to experiment with because sometimes half of the fish are in the thick stuff and half are on the edges," says Chapman.

The Kansas angler relies on a high-speed baitcast reel (7.1:1 gear ratio) to keep his toad buzzing over the weeds. Stout tackle is needed to winch fish out of the vegetation, so Chapman counts on a 7-foot, 2-inch heavy rod he normally uses for football jigs and magnum-sized plastic worms and fills his reel with 40- to 50-pound braid. "I definitely get better hooksets with the low stretch of braid, and when I get a fish on, a lot of times I am skiing those fish over the vegetation. So that braid with no line stretch helps win more of the battles."

Chapman will also buzz a toad whenever bass keep short-striking his buzz bait. If he notices fingerling shad in open water, Chapman opts for the toad rather than a buzz bait to mimic the baitfish and present a more subtle topwater offering.

Buzzing a plastic toad is a more subtle topwater presentation than a buzz bait for skittish bass in clear water.

70

Shallow Swimbait Tactics

The pros call it "throwing a sock" whenever they fish with the magnum-sized swimbaits.

The lures that started out as specialty baits for big bass in California have been downsized and mass produced to become one of the hottest baits in soft plastics.

FLW Tour pro Jay Yelas favors using a hollow-bodied swimbait in clear water when bass are ten feet deep or less. "It also really helps if there are a lot of baitfish up shallow that the bass are chasing," he suggests.

The tournament veteran believes the prime time to try a swimbait is after a shad spawn. "Typically that is a great time for a spinnerbait bite, but in clear water I know I can get seven to eight bites to one on a swimbait over a spinnerbait," reveals Yelas. The lure also produces for Yelas whenever he sees bass suspended in dock slips. He throws the swimbait into the wells and slowly swims it under the dock to trigger a strike from following fish.

The Oregon pro favors swimbaits in gizzard shad hues most of the time. "I choose my swimbait colors similar to how I choose spinnerbait skirt colors," he says. "The real loud whites and pearls work for me in the dirty water, and as I fish more clear water, I go to more translucent colors."

Yelas' favorite swimbait is packaged with a 6/0 weighted extra wide gap offset shank hook. "It is very important that you rig a swimbait just so the hook is in the exact middle of the bait," says Yelas, who rigs his swim baits Texas style. "If you don't get it in the middle, that bait will roll to one side or the other when you are reeling."

Retrieving the swimbait at a steady, slow to medium pace triggers the most strikes for Yelas.

A soft plastic swimbait is an effective lure for bass during the shad spawn.

71

Deep Swimbait Tricks

Most of today's swim baits are designed for fishing in shallow and mid-depths, but Texan Kelly Jordon has discovered that a heavily weighted swim bait can effectively probe deeper water.

The Bassmaster competitor throws a swimbait with an internal weight during the summer in deep water (eighteen to thirty-five feet) along the same type of structure where others throw deep-diving crankbaits. Jordon has caught fish on the swimbait at various lakes throughout the country by probing offshore structure such as points, channel drops, humps, and submerged pond dams. He prefers the weighted swimbait over a deep-diving crankbait because he believes the lure's single hook keeps the fish stuck better than the treble hooks of a crankbait.

Jordon's favorite presentation for summertime bass is a "burn-and-kill" retrieve. After letting the lure fall to the bottom, Jordon reels as fast as he can for five to ten cranks and then stops. He usually keeps his rod at the nine o'clock position, which puts him in a better stance for a quick hookset.

The presentation is similar to the jig-stroking tactic in which anglers jerk their rods high and hard to lift their lures off the bottom and let them fall on a slack line to trigger a strike. However, Jordon's technique keeps his rod in an ideal position for the hookset. "If you try to reel down when you feel a bite [on a slack line], most of the time the fish will have already dropped it," warns Jordon. "They hit the swimbait so aggressively, it's like they are trying to kill it."

If the "burn-and-kill" retrieve fails to produce, Jordon tries other presentations, such as dragging the lure along the bottom with short hops or slow rolling it and letting the bait occasionally fall back to the bottom.

Kelly Jordon throws a weighted swimbait in the summertime to catch bass along off-shore structure.

72

Hard Versus Soft Swimbaits

It's hard to keep a soft plastic swimbait on top and a hard plastic swimbait near the bottom, so the bass pros stock both versions of these lures in their boats.

Touring pros Ish Monroe, Byron Velvick, and Brent Ehrler opt for soft plastic models for most of their swimbait tactics, but they occasionally choose the hard plastic versions when bass are shallow or suspended high in the water column. "Those swimbaits basically address the water column from zero to five or ten feet," says Velvick. "It is a slow, shallow water bait. You can pause it; you can roll it slow; or you can work it like a Spook."

"About the only time I use a hard plastic swimbait is when I am fishing it as a topwater," says Ehrler. "When bass are on that topwater [swimbait], you can't beat it."

Hard swimbaits suspend better and have a unique action that Monroe employs for following fish. "When you are winding them and they are swimming through the water, if you get a fish to follow, you can snap the rod and the bait will do a 180-degree turn back around at the fish," says Monroe, "That triggers a lot of the fish into striking."

Monroe uses a soft swimbait most of the time because he says the fish "hold onto it a lot longer and seem to eat it a lot better." He notes the soft versions have better tail action and hookup ratios than the hard plastics. He also prefers the soft plastics for fishing in grass because the lures move through the vegetation better.

A soft swimbait's versatility permits Velvick to cover water quickly and fish the lure as deep as fifty feet. He also uses a soft plastic model when fishing around vegetation and trees because he can rig it weedless.

Hard swimbaits serve as excellent topwater lures, whereas soft swimbaits work more effectively in deeper water.

Pro anglers rely on soft plastics to catch bass, from the top of the water column to the bottom.

CHAPTER 7

Hard Baits

73

Jigs for All Seasons

While weather and water conditions constantly change throughout the year, bass fishing legend Denny Brauer's approach to catching bass rarely wavers.

Whether the skies are sunny or cloudy or if the water is low and clear or high and muddy, one certainty of any tournament is that Brauer will have a jig tied on at least one of his rods. "It is probably the most versatile bait in fishing," says Brauer of his confidence lure. "One of the main reasons I use it is because I like to catch big fish. I don't know of any other bait out there that appeals more to quality fish than a jig does."

A jig allows Brauer to slip the lure in and out of heavy cover easier than other lures. "It also hooks and holds a high percentage of fish to where you can land those bigger fish," he reveals.

An expert jig fisherman such as Brauer learns how to apply the lure under various conditions. "Take for instance in the fall when there are a lot of baitfish up and a lot of bass suspend on targets," says Brauer. "An angler who really hasn't spent a lot of time with a jig will pitch it out and let it go to the bottom. Then if he doesn't get a bite he'll try something else like a crankbait or spinnerbait. Whereas a guy who often fishes the jig realizes that if he starts swimming it, his lure is going to be in the same zone as the fish are and he is going to start generating some strikes."

Brauer varies the speed and motion of his retrieves depending on the seasons and the mood of the fish. In colder water, he fishes the jig at a slow, methodical pace; as the water warms up, Brauer speeds up his retrieves and imparts more erratic action to the lure.

Jig specialist Denny Brauer varies the speed and motion of his favorite lure to catch bass throughout all the seasons.

74

Cold and Hot Jig Tricks

Denny Brauer opts for a slow-falling jig and snail-pace retrieve during the pre-spawn when bass are still sluggish from the cold water. He creates the slow fall by matching a ¼- or ⅜-ounce jig with a plastic chunk trailer. Since he wants his lure to emulate a crawfish, Brauer opts for jig-and-chunk color combinations of chameleon craw and brown for clear water, black and blue in stained water, and black and chartreuse in muddy conditions.

Once his jig hits the bottom, Brauer crawls the lure by moving his rod tip in a motion similar to the standard plastic worm retrieve. He moves the jig four to six inches at a time while making sure the lure keeps contact with the bottom.

Cold water also prompts Brauer to take a slow approach when fishing a jig in cover. Sometimes the tournament veteran pitches his jig into a bush, lets it sit, and then shakes it in one place. "There are times when I actually dead stick it," he says. "I pitch it in there and don't move it."

Following the spawn, Brauer keys on bass along summertime structure and switches to a fast-falling jig. "If bass are relating to the bottom during the warmer months than I love to fish a heavy jig (½- to ¾-ounce) and I do a lot of hopping and sweeping it. Once you hop it up off the bottom, because it is a heavy jig, it will really pop off well and then it will fall real fast. Then you get the reflex strike out of those fish on the bottom."

The Texas pro sticks with the same crawfish-color jigs for his bottom-hopping tactics, but he changes trailers. Brauer opts for a plastic chunk with tantalizing kicking legs. "It makes the bait look like it's moving faster, like it's swimming," he describes.

When the weather warms up, Denny Brauer opts for a fast-falling jig to trigger reflex bites.

75

Swimming Jigs in Weeds

When bass tend to shy away from the flash and vibration of a spinnerbait running through the weeds, veteran tournament angler Dave Wolak recommends switching to a weedless jig and plastic trailer that has plenty of swimming action. His choice is a ¼-ounce jig featuring a retainer-guard on the jighead that allows Wolak to attach both the skirt and plastic trailer so the combo is more streamlined for gliding through the weeds.

"Three-eighths ounce [jig] is a little too heavy to get it going at a rate that a fish can eat it," Wolak says. "If you use a ⅛-ounce jig a lot of times it breaks off the water too much." Wolak's favorite trailer for his swimming jig is a 3 ¾-inch plastic craw.

The North Carolina pro makes his own skirts with silicone strands for his swimming jig. "I usually use a fluffier skirt," he says. "I will put on about four layers (about twelve strands per layer) on a swimming jig."

Most of the time Wolak uses a white jig tipped with a white trailer for his swimming tactics in the weeds during spring. However in low-light conditions or tannic water, he will switch to an all-black combo.

The former Bassmaster Classic qualifier adds action to his jig-and-craw combo with a constant rod movement. "I always keep my rod high and popping all the time," he says. "That makes the jig stay near the surface to where it will bulge the water and then dip down under."

Wolak likens this retrieve to waking a spinnerbait. "I am almost waking the jig; I feel I get more bites than I do if I have it at subsurface," he says. "If I can get the right retrieve so that it's just bulging the surface, I feel that the little bit of breaking the surface is what they want. They just can't handle that."

Dave Wolak triggers strikes from bass lurking in the weeds by swimming a jig along the vegetation.

76

Light Football Jigs for Spring

Bassmaster Elite Series competitor Brian Snowden throws a heavy football jig most of the year to catch bass on clear highland reservoirs, but in the spring he switches to the light version of the lure.

"The nice thing about using a lighter football jig is you can fish bigger rock and you don't get hung up as much," advises Snowden.

Throwing a ¾-ounce football jig produces best for Snowden when he targets deep bass, but when the fish move to the shallows to spawn, the Missouri angler opts for ⅜- and ½-ounce models of the bottom-bouncing bait.

The depth he's keying on determines which size jig Snowden selects for shallow bass. If the weather is calm and Snowden finds fish in the 5- to 10-foot depth range, he tosses a ⅜-ounce football jig, but when the wind blows hard and bass are holding in depths of ten to twenty feet, he opts for the ½-ounce model. While fishing pressure causes some anglers to scale down on the weight of their jigs, Snowden stays with the same size jig but downsizes the lure's profile by trimming the front and back of the jig's skirt.

Gravel or chunk rock bottoms are Snowden's top spots for delivering a football jig lite. "Most of the time when the fish are coming in to spawn, they will be on the chunk rock in the early spring, and then in the post-spawn, the fish will be on gravel points or underwater creek channels or ledges along a flat where they are still fairly shallow," he reveals.

Snowden makes short casts close to the bank and works the jig all the way back to the boat to cover different depths. Once he catches a few fish at a certain depth, he will position his boat five feet deeper and cast at 45-degree angles toward the bank.

Missouri pro Brian Snowden keys on gravel banks to drag lightweight football jigs along the bottom for springtime bass.

77

Slow-Rolling Spinnerbaits

The pre-spawn is Florida pro Bobby Lane's favorite time to tempt big bass with a magnum-blade spinnerbait worked slowly around any hydrilla, eelgrass, milfoil, pepper-grass, or lily pads he can find. "Those big pre-spawn females know where they want to go to spawn, but they just won't go up there yet because every third or fourth day a cold front approaches," Lane says. "So they will hold back. Well, every couple of days that go by, those big females have to eat. So when something big and slow comes by, that gets their attention."

Slow is the key word for this presentation. "The first thing you have to keep in mind in slow rolling a spinnerbait is the slower the better, but you also have to remember the blades do have to turn whether it's a big willowleaf or a Colorado," says Lane.

He throws a big Colorado in the dirty water and willowleaf blades more in the clear water. "Those big blades get their attention and have great vibration."

Lane throws a spinnerbait with a number five or six gold Colorado blade in murky water but switches to a silver willowleaf blade in the same sizes for clear water. He opts for a ⅜-ounce model for slow rolling in the shallows and a ½-ounce version for slowly winding in water deeper than five feet. His magnum-blade spinnerbaits for dirty and clear water also include a smaller trailing Colorado blade.

If he is fishing shallow wood or grass that tops out about two feet below the surface, Lane will start cranking his spinnerbait as soon as it hits the water. When concentrating on brush piles or other cover at depths of eight to ten feet, Lane lets his spinnerbait flutter down until it stops falling and then starts cranking just fast enough to feel the blade vibrating.

A willowleaf/Colorado blade combination works best for slow rolling spinnerbaits in clear water.

78

Summertime Spinnerbait Slinging

When the heat is on, one of the best spinnerbait slingers ever sticks with his blade bait.

While others opt for a plastic worm on a scorching summer day, Jimmy Houston slings his spinnerbait around shallow cover in murky water or deep weed edges in clear reservoirs.

The bass fishing legend throws his spinnerbait around any shallow cover such as logs, fence rows, brush piles, and stumps. A steady retrieve works best for Houston until his blade bait reaches a piece of cover. "I try to fish the lure as slowly as possible when I am in a potential strike zone, which is generally only a few inches on any given cast," he says. "When I get in that strike zone I will give a little shake or two with my rod tip or let that bait bump into the cover."

The Oklahoma pro keeps his rod pointed downward and moves it to the left or right at times to run his lure into the cover and trigger a reaction strike. "Not only do you have a deflection in the movement of the bait (when it hits the cover) you also have a deflection in the sound of the bait because the blade changes its rotation," he says.

Houston's favorite blade bait for shallow summertime fishing is a ½-ounce model (blue/chartreuse/white or fire tiger skirt) with a number five, six, or seven Oklahoma or Colorado blade.

If he's fishing a clear lake with deep grass, Houston switches to a ¾- or 1-ounce white spinnerbait with a number six or seven gold willowleaf blade and a number three silver Colorado blade.

Positioning his boat parallel to the weed line, Houston slow rolls the spinnerbait down to depths of ten to twenty feet. The key to his presentation is ticking the top of the grass throughout the retrieve.

TV show host and veteran tournament angler Jimmy Houston sticks with a spinnerbait in the summer for slinging around shallow cover.

79

Waking a Spinnerbait

BASS legend Rick Clunn lists waking a spinnerbait as his favorite way to catch bass because the high-speed retrieve triggers such vicious reflex strikes.

Although a fast pace is required for waking a blade bait, the speed of the retrieve must also be controlled. The key to the retrieve is to reel fast enough to make the blade wake the water behind it but not too fast to where the blade breaks the surface.

Combining the right lure weight and blade size is essential to waking a spinnerbait. "Any time you are waking, you have to maintain the balance between the pull of the blade and the weight of the head," says Clunn. "If the blade is too big it will overpower the head and try to pull it over." The Missouri pro suggests putting more weight on the head of the lure or switching to shorter blades if your spinnerbait continues to roll during a high-speed retrieve.

A spinnerbait can be waked with any type of blade, but Clunn prefers a unique spinner that he calls a long drop blade (a cross between an Indiana and a willowleaf blade). Clunn also favors a ¾-ounce spinnerbait because he believes the heavier lure tracks better in the water than the ½-ounce models most anglers use for waking.

The first step to waking a spinnerbait is to make a long cast to prevent spooking fish and trigger strikes at the far end of the presentation. Clunn begins his retrieve with his rod at the ten o'clock position and he continues to lower his rod as the lure gets closer to the boat. The lower rod angle prevents the spinnerbait from pulling up and keeps the blades from breaking the surface at the end of the retrieve. "The more it wakes all the way back the better off you are," Clunn concludes.

BASS legend Rick Clunn enjoys watching bass blast a waking spinnerbait.

80

Bottom-Bumping Crankbaits

When bass move into the 6- to 10-foot depth range in the spring and fall, Kevin VanDam selects a medium-diving crankbait to bounce along the bottom. A medium-diver also produces for VanDam in the summertime on lakes and rivers with stained to murky water.

"I love throwing those crankbaits around hard-bottom areas like rocks, riprap, and gravel or a lot of laydowns," says the BASS pro. "A mid-depth crankbait is also really good in grass lakes because a lot of grass lines run out to eight to ten feet and then stop, so a bait that runs six to eight feet is perfect for those situations."

For most of his crankbait tactics, VanDam wants a lure that is consistently hitting the bottom. "I want to have one that is running at its maximum depth just beyond the depth of that water," he says. "So if I am concentrating on that 6- to 10-foot zone, I want to have a bait that is going to run eight to eleven feet."

Varying his line size also helps VanDam bump the bottom with his crankbaits. He uses fluorocarbon line as heavy as 20-pound test to keep his crankbait running in the shallowest water and switches to 10-pound fluorocarbon when he wants his mid-depth crankbait to reach its maximum depth. "The difference between ten and twenty pounds is going to be several feet in running depth with the same bait," he says.

VanDam can also keep his mid-depth crankbaits constantly banging the bottom by varying his rod position. When the crankbait is close to the bank, VanDam keeps his rod tip high so the lure kicks bottom without hanging up. He continually lowers his rod as the crankbait runs along the bottom contour and points it straight down when the lure reaches its deepest point.

Bumping a mid-depth crankbait along rocky bottoms triggers strikes for Kevin VanDam in the spring and fall.

81

Kneeling and Reeling

His distinct kneel-and-reel form gives away what Paul Elias is doing in the summertime.

Despite the availability of longer rods, advancements in fishing lines, and crankbaits with capabilities to dive deeper, Elias still kneels down on the deck of his boat and sticks his rod in the water as he did in 1982 when he won the Bassmaster Classic. Holding his rod with all but the handle and reel under the water forced his deep-diving crankbait down to a submerged river bar that produced a Classic-winning weight of thirty-two pounds, eight ounces. "When you are trying to get a bait down eighteen to twenty feet, you just about have to kneel and reel if you want it down on the bottom for any amount of time," he says. "I want my bait digging into the bottom almost all of the time."

Long casts help Elias probe the bottom with his crankbait easier. "The longer cast you can make, the deeper you can get the bait and the quicker you can get it down," he says.

His favorite targets for deep cranking are shell beds ranging in depth from eight to twenty feet deep. The best beds are usually located along bars next to a creek or river channel. The Mississippi pro positions his boat to where he can cast his crankbait about twenty-five yards past the shell bed so his lure can reach its maximum depth at the right spot. "It takes a while for your bait to get down deep," he advises. "Your crankbait is usually at its deepest point when it is about two-thirds of the way back to the boat."

The former Bassmaster Classic champ triggers strikes by cranking his lure at a medium pace until it reaches its maximum depth, then he burns the lure to bang it into the bottom and frequently stops it.

To get his bait onto the bottom and keep it there as long as possible, Paul Elias relies on his kneel and reel tactic.

Allure of Lipless Crankbaits

The rattle of a lipless crankbait sounds like the ringing of a dinner bell to bass.

"One of the things that makes the lure such a good fish-catcher is that it is easy to use," says touring pro Kevin VanDam. "It is a lure you can fish all season long because it can be fished shallow and deep." The Michigan angler dotes on the lipless crankbait because its versatility allows him to use the lure in a variety of situations, such as covering long expanses of flats, running through schools of bass, busting the surface, or ripping through weeds.

VanDam favors throwing a ½-ounce lipless crankbait in the early spring and late fall when bass are shallow and the water temperature is in the 50-degree range.

Keeping the lure near the bottom is the key to VanDam's cold water presentation. "You want that bait skipping and clicking the rocks and the gravel if possible," he says. "I will slow it down enough to where I make sure it hits the bottom and then speed it up."

VanDam employs a pull-and-stop retrieve similar to a yo-yo presentation, but he keeps his rod down and pulls to the side rather than an overhead pull. "The great thing about that retrieve is that the lure will flutter down to the bottom when I let it fall," he says.

Relying on a low speed baitcast reel (5.3:1 gear ratio) helps VanDam slow down his retrieve and keeps the lure bouncing along the bottom. Most of the time he fills his reel with 10- to 12-pound test line to keep the crankbait running six to seven feet deep. When he wants to fish shallower, VanDam ties his lipless crankbait on 17-pound test so the buoyancy of the heavier line prevents the lure from digging the bottom and hanging up too much.

The versatility of a lipless crankbait allows Kevin VanDam to rip the lure through weeds or slowly bounce it along the bottom.

Suspending Stick Baits for Lunkers

Bassmaster pro Mike McClelland knows how lazy big bass can be, so he relies on a suspending stick bait because he can fish it slower and keep it in the strike zone longer than any other lure.

The suspending stick bait catches trophy fish because it produces best during late winter warming trends when pre-spawn heavyweight bass move up in the water column. McClelland's ideal conditions for throwing a stick bait are a sunny day with a light wind on a lake with slightly stained to clear water (visibility between one and a half to ten feet).

The Arkansas pro favors a suspending stick bait because he can effectively work it over any type of structure. "You can catch a lot of fish on a stick bait over open water. It is great when you have an isolated target, such as one standing tree on the end of a point, but it is also a bait that you can take off down a bank and cover a lot of water, whether it is deep or shallow."

McClelland notices many anglers make the mistake of twitching and jerking their bait as soon as it touches water.

"What you want to do though is, when that bait hits the water, just take eight or ten winds of the reel handle to get the bait down three or four feet," he says. Then McClelland pauses his retrieve, pulls the bait a few inches, and resumes with sequences of twitch-twitch-pause.

Patience is a virtue with this tactic since it sometimes requires prolonged pauses. "I don't feel like you can ever let the bait sit too long," says McClelland. "If you have the bait in a prime target area, the longer you can let it sit there the better your chances of catching that fish that is not really in that good of a mood to eat."

A suspending stick bait is Mike McClelland's favorite lure for coaxing lethargic largemouth into biting during the wintertime.

84

Vertical Spooning

Bass fishing in the cold is hard on the old bones, but it is definitely more soothing for your casting shoulder.

When bass go deep in the winter, long casts are usually unnecessary, since most of the action will be right below the boat. So most savvy bass anglers break out the light line and drop their lures straight down to reach bass hugging the bottom or suspended over deep structure. Vertical presentations for wintertime bass require a heavy enough lure for probing deep, so a jigging spoon becomes a go-to lure throughout the cold months.

Since bass feed on small shad during early winter, Alabama pro Gerald Swindle matches the forage by vertically presenting a ¼-ounce jigging spoon. The lure produces largemouth bass holding at depths of twenty to twenty-five feet on most of the reservoirs Swindle fishes in the winter.

Swindle prefers a chrome jigging spoon or a white model, which he modifies by replacing the original hook with a white feathered number four treble hook. He prefers the spoon over soft plastics for vertical jigging because he can work it faster and cover more of the water column quicker.

"If you hop it in a school of bass you are going to get a strike," says Swindle. "I can trigger them into biting on it even if the fish aren't feeding."

The touring pro vertical jigs his spoon with a 6-foot, 10-inch medium casting rod and baitcast reel filled with 12-pound fluorocarbon line. Swindle starts his presentation with his rod held at ten o'clock and jerks it to twelve o'clock a couple of times before slowly lowering it to follow the fall of the spoon. "I kind of hop it twice off the bottom about twelve to fifteen inches and then let it fall back to the bottom," says Swindle.

Vertical jigging a slab spoon is an effective tactic for staying on top of a school of wintertime bass.

(Illustration courtesy of Rod Walinchus)

85

Tight-Lining Tailspinners

When shad move to the steep cuts in the backs of creeks during autumn, Missouri angler Brian Snowden tricks bass with a tailspinner. "I like it because I can feel the blade turn and the big key is, when fishing that bait, you can actually feel it hit those schools of shad and kind of bounce around," he says. "With that tail spinning, you can keep kind of a tight line on it and feel it as it is working. Then if that tail stops or you don't feel it anymore, you need to set the hook because nine out of ten times the bite is going to come when that bait is falling."

Once the lure falls through the shad, Snowden lifts the tailspinner back up to the shad and lets it fall again to mimic an injured baitfish that has been hammered by bass slamming through the baitfish pods. He keeps his medium-heavy rod high (noon to one o'clock position) and lets the lure fall on a semi-taut line so it drops straight down rather than pendulums.

The Bassmaster pro selects a ½-ounce tailspinner when the baitfish are suspended ten to twenty feet deep in the early fall, but he switches to a ¾-ounce model when the water gets colder and the shad drop deeper. His favorite color combination is white with a gray back, but he opts for a model with some chartreuse on it if the weather is overcast. The only modification he makes to the bait is to replace the original treble hook with a larger treble (usually number four) to get better hookups.

"This is a quality fish technique," says Snowden, who works the tailspinner on 17-pound test fluorocarbon. "You are not going to get a lot of bites in a day, but you are going to catch 3- to 5-pound fish doing this."

A tailspinner produces for Brian Snowden when bass suspend under baitfish in the cuts of creeks during early fall.

86

Speeding up Spooks

The tantalizing slow zigzag of a walking topwater bait such as a Heddon Zara Spook usually triggers strikes, but Texan Zell Rowland sometimes turns up the speed on his topwater offerings, especially in the fall to mimic fleeing shad.

"That time of the year, bass have a tendency to be chasing a lot of baitfish," he says. "When I see that kind of activity, I want my bait to match what those fish are looking at."

The tournament veteran fires his Zara Spook past any busting activity he spots and proceeds to jerk the lure at an extremely fast pace. "It will sort of walk from side to side, but instead of the bait having an 80- to 90-degree turn, it will have about a 10-degree or less turn," Rowland says. "It almost looks like the bait is coming straight at you without any side movement."

The size of the topwater plug he uses depends on the fishery and conditions. If he is fishing a lake known for its big bass, Rowland opts for the 5-inch Super Spook; but for fisheries filled with smaller bass, he chooses the original 4 ½-inch Spook. The smaller Super Spook Junior (three and a half inches) works best on pressured waters. He also notes the smaller Spook is easier to control when he employs the faster retrieve. Rowland's tackle for his high-speed topwater tactic includes a 6-foot, 8-inch medium-light casting rod and a 6.1:1 gear ratio baitcast reel filled with 17- or 20-pound copolymer monofilament.

The Texas pro usually finds bass busting shad along points near the backs of creeks during the fall. Rowland casts his lure past the busting activity since he knows a bass is on the move and will no longer be in the spot where it surfaced. He fan casts around the surface activity trying to pinpoint the direction the foraging bass are heading.

Twitching a Zara Spook at a fast pace tricks busting bass in the fall.

(Photo courtesy of Lawrence Taylor)

87

Popping a Topwater

Considered a maestro of the topwater popper, Zell Row-land has been credited with the revival of the Rebel Pop-R and creation of the Zell Pop. Whereas the Pop-R was designed as a chugger that Rowland modified to pop and spit, the Zell Pop was created specifically to spit and sound like a shad flicking across the surface.

The topwater spitter produces best for Rowland when shad are in the shallows spawning and in any waters that contain a large shad population. The BASS pro prefers throwing the Zell Pop in clearer water because of the lure's spitting ability. In dirty-water situations, he opts for the Pop-R since it creates more noise to attract bass hampered by the low-visibility conditions.

Rowland also bases his lure choice on the speed of the retrieve he will employ rather than the slickness or rough-ness of the water. When he wants to retrieve a topwater at high speed and cover a lot of water, Rowland selects the spitter, and if he needs to work his lure slowly and keep it close to a target, he prefers the popper.

"I pretty much let a fish tell me how much action it wants out of a bait; when I learn that, then that is pretty much what

I will go with," says Rowland. "I usually start out fishing the bait fairly slow, where I might twitch it two or three times, then let it hesitate and twitch it once or twice. If that is not very productive I might move the bait four to six feet instead of three feet at a time."

Rowland twitches his topwater poppers on monofilament line ranging from 12- to 17-pound test. "Line size is a big key for any topwater bait that you throw," says Rowland. "Usually as a rule of thumb, the lighter the line the more action you get."

Zell Rowland tinkers with his topwater plugs to make the lures spit or pop.

88

100-Degree Topwaters

A topwater plug is probably one of the last lures most bass anglers choose for 100-degree days, but it's a top choice for Texas pro Zell Rowland.

The Bassmaster Elite Series competitor catches bass in the shallows or over deep water in the summertime heat with a Heddon Zara Spook or a Rebel Pop-R. "Every lake that you go to, there are always fish that are going to be in shallow water depending on the types of cover available," says Rowland. "The best cover will be docks or lay-down logs that cast shade, where the water will be cooler. Usually in the very hot summertime, I might be in four feet of water going down the bank throwing a topwater bait and working it fast."

High-speed topwater tactics also produce on a deep, clear reservoir. "When the temperature out there is 100 to 110 degrees, we wear out the fish throwing a Zara Spook or a Pop-R over twenty-five to thirty feet of water," he says. "We can work those lures as fast as we can to trigger strikes."

Water clarity determines how fast Rowland starts working his topwaters. "Generally the clearer the water the faster I will work it, but the more color the water has, the more I slow the bait down."

Rowland can make his Zara Spook move side to side at high speeds by rapidly working it on 17- to 20-pound line. The Texas pro employs the same steady fast-paced retrieve with a Pop-R to make the lure spit water rather than pop on the surface.

If a bass strikes and misses his lure, Rowland either keeps working the lure at the same pace or stops it. He knows that the fish is usually watching for the lure's next move, so he provokes a strike by nudging a Pop-R forward to makes its tail feathers flare.

Topwater expert Zell Rowland still tries a surface popper for bass when the thermometer tops 100 degrees.

(Photo by Lawrence Taylor)

89

Understanding Buzz Baits

Few fishing thrills match the excitement of watching a buzz bait suddenly disappear when a bass engulfs it, yet some anglers shun the lure because it is one of the most misconceived baits in their tackle box. "Some people just think it is a morning and evening lure," says Bassmaster Elite Series pro Brent Chapman. "I think that is one of the biggest misconceptions about topwater fishing. Some of the best topwater fishing is during the midday."

The Kansas pro favors throwing a buzz bait in the fall in stained to dirty water. "The fish are more in that strike zone of five feet or less and are more apt to eat a buzz bait," says Chapman, "whereas in the summertime the majority of the fish are deeper."

As the water temperature continues to cool, some anglers stop throwing the buzzer, which Chapman believes is a mistake. "I think we all have the misconception that when the water drops in to the upper fifties that the fish get off the buzz bait," says Chapman who has caught bass when the water temperature was in the forties and it was snowing. "You just have to keep it in your arsenal and be willing to try it."

Chapman's favorite target for buzzing in the shallows is some type of aquatic vegetation, such as milfoil or hydrilla. "I get awfully excited when I see a nice brush pile, laydown, or dock too," he says.

A medium-paced, steady retrieve triggers strikes most of the time for Chapman. "Sometimes I like to throw it out, pop it, reel it, then kill it for a split second, and then just keep reeling it," he says.

For most situations, he selects a ⅜- or ½-ounce model, although he switches to a ⅛-ounce buzzer when fishing clear water or heavily pressured bass.

A buzz bait triggers strikes any time bass are cruising in the shallows.

90

Early Start on Buzzing

During the spring, Texan Zell Rowland is an early bird who gets bass on the surface. "I like throwing a top-water bait when the water temperature gets about 50 to 55 degrees," he says. "That is pretty cold, but I have seen fish caught in tournaments on buzz baits when the water temperature was forty-eight."

The Texas pro favors a buzz bait in the early spring when the fish are in the pre-spawn stage and are suspending in shallower water. A couple of warm, sunny days draw some of these pre-spawn bass into the 3- to 5-foot depth range where Rowland can coax the fish to the surface with his topwater presentation.

The back ends of main lake pockets are Rowland's favorite spots to throw topwaters in the early spring because these areas warm up quicker than the main lake. He also targets pockets on the northern side of a lake, which receive more exposure to the sun.

The speed of Rowland's buzzer presentation is critical during the early spring. "A rule of thumb is that, usually when the water temperature is very cool like that, the fish are very sluggish, so you have to fish a buzz bait much slower," he says.

While others might consider a buzz bait too fast for sluggish, pre-spawn bass, Rowland knows he can slow down his blade bait with some tinkering. Bending the cups of the lure's blades inward allows Rowland to creep the buzzer across the surface. The topwater expert suggests that this modification also changes the sound of the buzzer to coax fish to the top.

If the water continues to warm up throughout the day, Rowland makes another adjustment to increase the speed of his buzz bait. The BASS pro will open the cups of the lure's blade to make his buzzer move faster.

Buzz baits in the early spring coax quality bass to the surface.

91

Chattering Baits for Bass

The design of the Original Chatterbait prompted several lure manufacturers to create bladed swim jigs, combining the compact profile of a jig with the flash of a spinnerbait and the vibration of a square-bill crankbait.

"The front blade pushes a lot of water around, so the fish can feel it and hear it because it makes a little clicking sound as it is being retrieved," says Bassmaster competitor Stephen Browning. "When bass are feeding on shad or bream I will have one tied on."

The Arkansas pro usually throws a Chatterbait in the spring when bass are on beds and during the shad spawn. He prefers Chatterbaits in bluegill hues to mimic the sunfish that bass are constantly chasing away from their nests and switches to lures in shad colors when the baitfish are spawning in late spring or early summer. Since spawning shad are usually larger, Browning tips his Chatterbait with a soft jerk bait to match the size of the baitfish.

When he wants to fish his blade bait near the surface, Browning opts for a ¼-ounce Original Chatterbait. Adding a plastic craw with paddle-style pinchers as a trailer also helps Browning run his blade bait slower yet keep it closer to the surface. He chooses a ⅜-ounce Chatterbait for running in deeper water, and runs both size baits on 16-pound fluorocarbon line with a 7-foot medium-heavy rod and 6.4:1 baitcast reel.

Bass crave the action, noise, and shape of a bladed swim jig.

When the pros want versatility from a lure, they usually opt for a hard bait, such as a crankbait, spinnerbait, or jig.

CHAPTER 8

Bass Knots

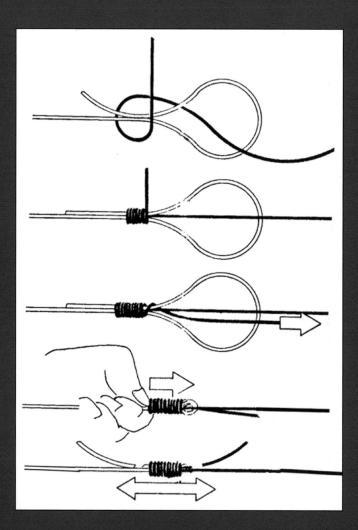

San Diego Jam Knot

Beginning anglers usually learn to tie a line directly to the lure with an improved clinch knot. However, Virginia pro John Crews prefers the stronger San Diego Jam Knot for cinching monofilament or fluorocarbon line directly to his baits. "I have tested it on the knot machines and it is just as strong as the Trilene, Palomar, or any other knot," says Crews.

The four steps for tying this knot are the following:

1. Thread the line through the line tie.
2. Loop the tag end over your index finger and wrap it four times around the loop towards the eye. Slip the tag end through the loop near the line tie and bring it back to the loop around your index finger.
3. Thread the tag end through the loop and remove your finger.
4. Wet the lines and pull the tag end tight. Push the knot tight to the line tie and trim the tag end.

San Diego Jam Knot.

93

Double-Strength Palomar

Since he considers the Palomar knot to be the strongest knot he can tie, BASS pro Stephen Browning ties this knot on all of his lures. He believes that the doubling of the line through the eye of the lure is what makes this knot so strong. "There is a lot of stress where the eye of a bait meets the line, and I think if you have double line there, it tends not to wear down the line as much as a single loop," says Browning.

The steps for tying a Palomar knot are the following.

1. Double the line to form a loop and pass the loop's end through the eye of the hook.
2. Form an overhand knot with the standing line by holding it between your thumb and finger and grasping the loop with your free hand.
3. Slip the hook through the loop and tighten the line while guiding the loop over the top of the eyelet. Browning suggests wetting the line during this step to lessen friction when the lines rub together.
4. Steadily pull the tag end of the line tight to the eyelet and trim off the tag end.

Palomar Knot.

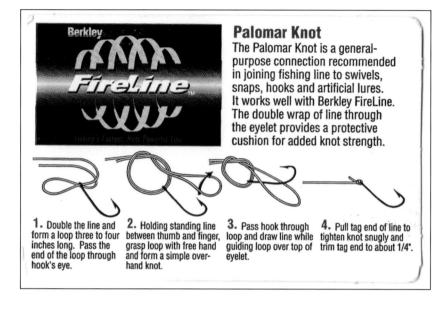

Palomar Knot

The Palomar Knot is a general-purpose connection recommended in joining fishing line to swivels, snaps, hooks and artificial lures. It works well with Berkley FireLine. The double wrap of line through the eyelet provides a protective cushion for added knot strength.

1. Double the line and form a loop three to four inches long. Pass the end of the loop through hook's eye.

2. Holding standing line between thumb and finger, grasp loop with free hand and form a simple overhand knot.

3. Pass hook through loop and draw line while guiding loop over top of eyelet.

4. Pull tag end of line to tighten knot snugly and trim tag end to about 1/4".

94

Non-slip Loop Knot

Popularized by fishing legend Lefty Kreh, this loop knot, also known as the "Kreh Loop," gives a lure more natural action than the same bait attached to a lock snap or snap swivel. Bassmaster pro John Crews employs this knot whenever he ties a large- to medium-sized topwater popper with monofilament line ranging from 14- to 20-pound test. "It works best with big line for getting a lot of action out of a smaller bait," he says.

The knot can be tied in three steps:

1. Start with an overhand knot and pass the tag end through the line tie and back through the loop of the overhand knot.
2. Wrap the tag end around the main line four times and slip the tag end back through the overhand knot.
3. Wet the knot and slowly pull on the tag end to cinch the wraps together. Then pull the loop and main line in opposite directions to finish the knot. Trim the tag end.

Loop knot.

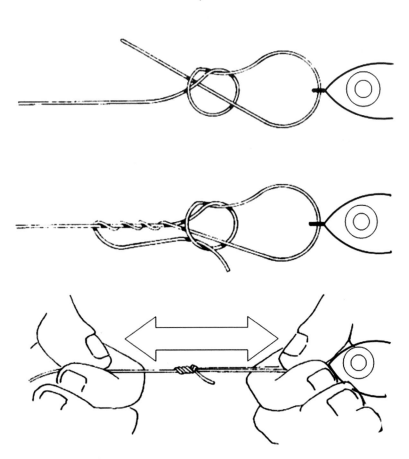

95

Two-Line Connection

When FLW competitor Glenn Browne needs to tie a fluorocarbon leader to his main braid line, he relies on a modified Albright knot known as the Alberto knot. He prefers this connection because it is a small, strong knot that glides easily through both conventional and micro-rod guides. The knot allows Browne to tie a leader of 6- to 10-pound fluorocarbon to braided line ranging from 15- to 50-pound test for his finesse fishing tactics.

Here's how to tie an Alberto knot:

1. Form a loop with the fluorocarbon leader and hold it between your thumb and forefinger.
2. Insert the braided line through the loop and wrap it around the loop at least six times.
3. Switch hands and wrap the braid back toward the entry point of the loop with the same amount of loops as you used in Step 2. Pass the braid back out of the loop in the same direction as you started.
4. Wet and hold all four lines at the same time and slowly push the braided wraps to the middle of the leader loop. Make sure none of the braid loops roll on top or over the other braid loops. Snug the knot and snip the tag lines of the fluorocarbon and braid.

Alberto Knot.

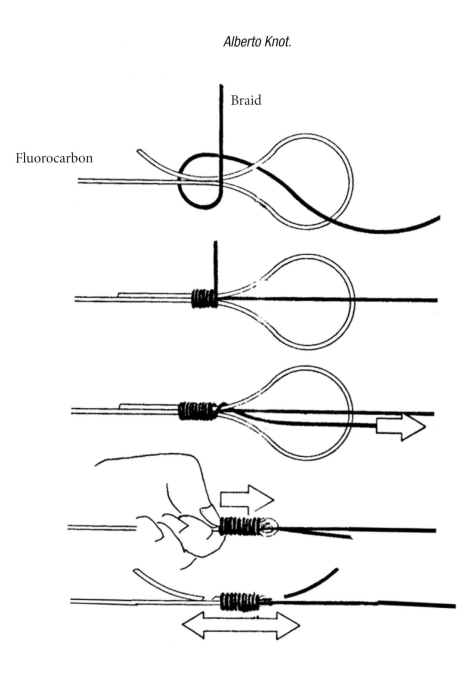

Braid

Fluorocarbon

The pros know a strong knot is the key to winning their battle with a bass.

CHAPTER 9

Bass Homework

96

Researching Unfamiliar Waters

When Alton Jones attended college, his study habits got sidetracked.

"I did as little of my homework as I could to get by," he recalls. Now that he fishes for a chance to win a top prize of $100,000 or more, Jones has plenty of incentive to do his homework.

Homework becomes especially important to Jones when he sees new fisheries on the tournament schedule. Before he can start formulating a plan for unfamiliar waters, Jones goes online to gather information about the fishery. His first step is to research tournament results. "The first thing I am going to do is find out what I need to be catching to win and what I need to catch to do well. I want to know where the bar is set and what the winning weight on that lake is usually." Tournament results also give him some insight on which sections of a lake produce the biggest stringers.

Other details he gathers from the Internet include the lake level history and the long-term weather trends for the area. By researching the weather patterns for a couple of months, Jones can determine if the lake is in extended drought conditions that push the fish offshore or if torrential rains and warmer-than-normal weather has kept the fish shallow. Surfing the web can also provide clues about the lake's water clarity.

Map reading is the second step of Jones' research on unfamiliar waters. Laying a paper map on his bed and looking at it from a distance helps Jones quickly determine the largest areas of deep and shallow waters and how the river channel winds through the reservoir.

Studying his paper and electronic maps can help Jones target the areas he plans on fishing based on the time of year the tournament will be held.

Alton Jones does his homework on the Internet and with maps when researching unfamiliar waters.

(Photo courtesy of Lawrence Taylor)

97

Predicting Seasonal Patterns

Mike Iaconelli's preparations for a Bassmaster Classic on the Louisiana Delta illustrates how much time and effort the pros put into researching the bodies of water they will be fishing in upcoming tournaments.

For six and a half months, Iaconelli followed the same two-part process he uses for Elite Series events. The New Jersey pro started preparing for the Classic at home by researching the Louisiana Delta through back issues of magazines, Internet websites of fish and game agencies, and local contacts. Rather than collecting waypoints from local anglers, Iaconelli keyed on generalities of the fishery and "buzz words" from about two dozen sources. When key words about lure colors, water clarity, vegetation, or sections of the Delta kept popping up, Iaconelli would jot down these buzz words in his notes.

His next research step involved plugging a formula he calls General Universal Seasonal Patterns (GUSP) into his maps. "It is kind of a template that tells me where the bass are going to live based on the seasonal pattern," he says. "Wherever you are at, a bass is a bass and it goes through certain things during its life cycle of the four seasons. So based on that template, I knew that when we got to the Louisiana Delta on the third week of February, the fish were going to be in the wintering mode or the pre-spawn mode depending on current weather conditions."

The research and GUSP template helped Iaconelli eliminate water before he got to the Delta. "So it took a place that was 500,000 fishable acres and I could reduce it 20,000 acres," says Iaconelli.

Iaconelli spent two months of his research time for the Classic building a map base on the Delta. His sources included the Army Corps of Engineers, National Oceanic and Atmospheric Administration (NOAA), Navionics map downloads, and post-Hurricane Katrina aerial maps.

Mike Iaconelli relies on magazine articles, websites of game and fish agencies, and local contacts to research future tournament sites on his busy schedule.

(Photo courtesy of Berkley)

98

Keep Electronics Simple

FLW competitor Mark Rose has a suggestion for copy writers of manuals for fishing electronics. "I think the manual should be one page that says you ought to leave the unit just like it is," says Rose.

"One of the biggest mistakes people make is getting too complicated with their electronics by setting their sensitivity a certain way or their kilohertz a certain way or trying to zoom in too much," Rose says. "Ninety-nine percent of the time I use my unit just the way it is with the factory settings. So factory settings will usually get you where you need to be."

The Arkansas pro suggests there are certain situations where an angler might need to adjust the settings. "I will strengthen my sensitivity a little bit if I have lots of real high waves or if there are just so many shad that I can't see through them," he says. "I also have to adjust [the sensitivity] a lot of times when I get into tannic water in Florida." He suggests turning down the sensitivity when encountering high waves or massive schools of shad that prevent the unit from displaying a bottom reading. Rose recommends increasing the unit's sensitivity for fishing in deep water (thirty feet or deeper).

Mark Rose relies on the factory settings of his fishing electronics in most situations to pinpoint bass or fish-attracting structure.

99

Side-Imaging Settings

Remember when guys were all hush-hush about their hotspots during conversations at the bait-and-tackle shop?

Those guys kept a code of silence like they were protecting some national security secret, but side-imaging technology has made it easier and quicker for pros and amateurs alike to reveal all those secret hotspots.

"The biggest advantage to side imaging is just covering water," says Bassmaster pro Terry Scroggins. "It works best in shallow-water situations as far as being able to cover more territory, because the traditional sonar unit that shoots down starts off with a beam the size of a dollar piece at the transducer puck and goes out at about a 45-degree angle: the shallower the water the less angle you see the bottom. Side imaging shoots out there no matter whether it is three feet, five feet, twenty-five feet, or thirty feet. You see out there however far you want to see."

Scroggins turns off the auto feature of his side-imaging unit and adjusts the sensitivity. When he is scanning in eight to fifteen feet of water, Scroggins set his sensitivity at about twelve and will increase it to fourteen for scanning in deeper water.

The Florida pro prefers keeping his side-imaging range setting between forty and sixty feet to get the most detailed side view. "You can set it at 150 feet but you can't tell what anything is," he says.

The screen display on side-imaging units offers a variety of color backgrounds. Scroggins prefers the brown palette, which he believes brings out more detail.

Idling at certain speeds also gives Scroggins the best images while side scanning. Going too slow or too fast muddles the picture. "I like to go from an idle to no more than six miles per hour," says Scroggins, who suggests three to four miles per hour probably produces the best results.

Side-imaging electronics allow anglers to scan areas on both sides of a boat to find bass hideouts quicker.

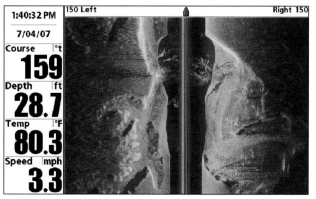

(Image courtesy of Jim Edlund)

The most successful anglers on the tournament trail spend countless hours consulting their electronics while practicing on unfamiliar waters.

CHAPTER 10

Furthering Your Bass Education

100

Back to School

The College of Hard Knocks has been the learning center for many of the pros on the Bassmaster and FLW tournament trails.

Some of these pro anglers who learned the hard way are offering higher learning opportunities to their fans by conducting various on-the-water classes and classroom courses. Fishing professors include Mike Iaconelli, Pete Gluszek, Mark Menendez, and Guido, Dion, and Payden Hibdon.

Iaconelli and FLW Tour pro Pete Gluszek have teamed up to conduct the Bass University—a series of classroom sessions taught by Bassmaster and FLW Tour pros at various locations throughout the country. "We get guys who are winning tournaments right now and give them an open forum to speak about their strengths," says Gluszek. "We also tailor our speakers to the region we visit."

Western Kentucky Community and Technical College hosts a Bass Fishing Class with Menendez as the instructor. "It is an in-depth look at seasonal patterns and techniques," says Menendez, who holds his class in the winter.

The Hibdon's School of Fishing features FLW pros Guido, Dion, and Payden Hibdon. The two-day courses held on weekends in the spring and fall at Lake of the Ozarks cover a wide variety of topics including boat positioning, line and lure choices, reading weather patterns, and effective ways to practice for a tournament.

Other excellent venues for learning about bass fishing are the seminars conducted by the top pros at various sports shows and sporting goods stores throughout the country.

Mike Iaconelli conducts a classroom session of the Bass University.

(Photo by Bill Decoteau)

101

Learn from a Bass Club

Many bass anglers have been introduced to their favorite pastime by a relative or friend. However, when novices or even some seasoned anglers want to advance to a higher level of the sport, they join a bass club.

Long before he became a superstar on the tournament trail, Kevin VanDam honed his skills in a bass club. "The fastest way to learn in bass fishing is to fish with as many good fishermen as you can," he says. "The more different things you see done by a knowledgeable fisherman the better your chances of being successful out there on the water. The bass club is the perfect scenario for that situation.

"When I joined a bass club, [the learning process] was never ending," VanDam recalls. "We had guys who were really good finesse fishermen or deep-water grub fishermen, and I learned those tactics from them. I also learned how to be a good shallow-water slop fisherman. I learned a lot of techniques—like flipping—that I didn't have any experience in at all."

Clubs can be found just about anywhere in the United States. "In most clubs you fish with a different club member at a handful of lakes over a season," says VanDam. "That is the kind of club you should look for. You don't want to fish a club where you fish with one team guy all the time, because all you learn is what each of you know or what you learn together out there on the water."

VanDam suggests that a club is a great avenue for anglers who want to fish from a bass boat but can't afford to own one yet. The Michigan pro also notes that a club provides non-boaters on-the-water experience with boats and equipment, such as trolling motors and electronics.

Competing in club tournaments is the quickest way to learn about bass fishing from a variety of experienced anglers.

Index